Burke Hinsdale

The Jewish-Christian church

Burke Hinsdale

The Jewish-Christian church

ISBN/EAN: 9783337102234

Printed in Europe, USA, Canada, Australia, Japan

Cover: Foto ©Lupo / pixelio.de

More available books at **www.hansebooks.com**

Entered according to Act of Congress, in the Year 1878, by
B. A. HINSDALE,
In the Office of the Librarian of Congress at Washington, D. C.

The chapters comprising this little book were originally written as parts of a much more ambitious work. A variety of causes brought that work to a stand-still several years ago, and it is doubtful when it will be completed, if at all. I send them out in this form, believing that they have a center of unity, and also that they will prove serviceable to students of the Bible, and of Church History and Theological Science. There can be no greater errors than these: "The Bible can be understood as an unrelated fact, separate from the general history of the world"; and "the History of the Church can be grasped simply by knowing what is going on in the homes and public meetings of Christians." Both the Scriptures and Church History are parts of the History of the Race, and they must be taken in their historical connections. He has studied the Bible to little purpose (other than a moral one) who has not learned to watch the currents of events and thoughts that move behind the page—that is, has not learned to read between the lines. To get into the minds of men who lived so long ago as the primitive Christians is difficult, but I hope I have not wholly failed in my attempt.

HIRAM, O., July 8, 1878.

TABLE OF CONTENTS

FIRST PART.

...E FEATURES OF JEWISH...

- ...ONDITIONS OF GROWTH.
- ...WO ELEMENTS OF CIV...
- ...E LAW.
- ...E PRIESTHOOD.
- ...E PROPHETS.
- ...BBINISM.
- ...LLENISM.
- ...CAPITULATION.

SECOND PART.

...HE JEWISH-CHRISTIAN CHUR...

- ...—INTRODUCTION.
- II.—BEFORE PENTECOST.
- III.—JERUSALEM AND JUDEA.
- IV.—SAMARIA.
- V.—THE CONVERSION OF CORNELIUS.
- VI.—THE CONVERSION OF GREEKS IN ANTIOCH.
- VII.—THE COUNCIL OF JERUSALEM.
- VIII.—THE MINISTRY OF PAUL.
- IX.—THE CATASTROPHE.
- X.—SUMMARY AND CONCLUSION.

NOTE.—F. C. BAUER'S THEORIES.

PART FIRST.

FEATURES OF JEWISH CUL[TURE]

[N]... prepared to study the history... [Jewi]sh
Chr[istian]... who has not a knowledge of s[ome] ...[featur]es
of J[ewish cu]lture. This will be readily ad[mitted, n]or
can [he be p]repared to study that history, [and] to
und[erstand t]he effect produced upon the G[entile by] its
Jewi[sh envir]onment, unless he has paid some [attention] to
the e[ffect of] conditions in general. This fact [is excu]se
for d[evoting] a few pages to that subject.

I.—CONDITIONS OF GROWTH.

There has been much dispute over the question, What is a cause? It answers my purpose to say that a cause is "operating power;" or, more strictly, "power which in operating originates new forms of being." Happily the definition of a condition is less in dispute. It is defined to be "That which is attendant on the cause, or co-operates with it for the accomplishment of the result, or that which limits the cause in its operation." A condition proper is never a cause, but the cause of any phenomenon is also one of its conditions, as we shall soon see.

The conditions of an evolution are various; some of them internal, others external. The most important is the germ from which the evolution is produced. By no process of fish-culture can you produce a fish from the egg of a[...] nor by any process of tree-culture, a maple from the [...] of an oak. Why this is so—why the germ is the impo[rtant] factor in all growth—is one of the mysteries of life [not] yet explained. It is quite true that the germ is the ca[use,] or one cause, of the growth; it is also a condition, sin[ce it] serves to determine the character of the growth. But [the] germ is not the only condition of life. External facts, w[hile] they do not, so far as has been shown, change the esse[ntial] character of any form of life, do change many of its p[rop]erties. Food, shelter, and selection in breeding are po[tent] factors in the growth of an animal; and soil, temperat[ure,] the rain-supply, etc., tell powerfully on the growth [of a] plant. The history of animals and plants under domes[tica]tion contains a vast body of the most curious and instr[uct]ive facts, showing how man, by the selection of bree[ding] animals and the choice of seeds, as well as by chan[ging] external conditions, modifies animal and plant-life. [A] London correspondent of an American journal a few [years] ago described a novel exhibition which he attended i[n the] Crystal Palace, viz: of birds. It was a prize exhibi[tion] and was the means of bringing together some thousan[ds of] rare and curious specimens, many of which were the [result] of the British bird-fancier's art. In his own words:

"The majority are canaries, and it is wonderful what variety has [been] secured in the culture of this little bird. From little brown t[hings] hardly bigger than a large-sized moth, to burly yellow creatures, [big] as a swallow, we have every dimension and every variation of colo[r and] plumage. A prize having been offered for the most eccentri[cally] colored canary, we have the drollest arrangement of dyes—som[e] yellow on one side and dark on the other, others striped like little z[ebras,] others spotted." One canary has a "note just like the sound of the [G] string of a violin; others are as mellow-toned as a German flute."*

A still more striking illustration of the same so[rt is] furnished by the natural history of pigeons. It is

---

* M. D. Conway in *Cincinnati Commercial.*

common opinion of naturalists that the different breeds of the pigeon are descended from the *Columba livia*, or rock pigeon; yet the diversity of the existing varieties is justly said to be something extraordinary. The carrier, especially the male bird, is remarkable for the development of corniculated skin about the head, accompanied by elongated eyelids, large external nostrils, and a wide gaping mouth; the short-faced tumbler has a face almost like that of a finch; the runt is of great size, with long, massive beak and feet, some of the sub-breeds having very long necks, others very long wings and tails; the barb, though like the carrier in some respects, differs from him in having a short, broad beak; the pouter has an enormously developed crop, which it is very fond of inflating; the turbit, a line of reversed feathers down the breast; the jacobin wears a hood of feathers on the back of the neck; the trumpeter and laugher differ from all other pigeons in their coo; the fantail has thirty or forty tail feathers instead of twelve or fourteen, the normal number in the pigeon family, and these are kept so expanded that the head and tail touch.* Hence a great fancier of pigeons, Sir John Sebright, was accustomed to say "he would produce any given feather in three years, but it would take him six years to obtain head and beak." A great authority, speaking of what breeders have done for sheep, says: "It would seem that they had chalked upon a wall a form perfect in itself and then given it existence." Still another authority, Youatt, describes the principle of selection as "the magician's wand" by means of which the breeder "may summon into life whatever form or mould he pleases."† It is true that these facts relate to organic life in an artificial state, but nature abounds in similar facts showing the power of external conditions over all forms of life.

---

* See *The Origin of Species*, by Chas. Darwin, New York, 1871, pp. 33–4.
† Herbert Spencer, *Biology*, New York, 1866, Vol. I. p. 242.

The examples given above find their analogues in human life, in its physical, intellectual, and moral aspects. Confining my remarks to the two latter, each individual brings into the world a certain amount of positive character; but he is more or less modified by the various forces that play upon him from without. "Imagine all the infants born this year in Boston and Timbuctoo to change places!" says the Autocrat of the Breakfast-Table.* To what extent man's will makes him superior to circumstances, and therefore a *center*stance, is an interesting philosophical question; but it cannot be here discussed. Nor need we inquire how far the analogies of nature hold in the realm of history; it is enough to know that general conditions do profoundly influence individual and collective humanity. We can never understand a man unless we take him in relation to his home, his history, and the age in which he lives; nor can we understand the genesis and character of the science, philosophy, literature, and religion of a people, if we divorce these aspects of its life from physical and historical facts.

The different Christian theologies are their authors' apprehensions of Christianity, cast in the forms of philosophy.

The principal factor in the history of Christian doctrine has been, emphatically, Christianity itself. No one can carefully study the subject without being impressed by that fact. For myself, I have sometimes found Christianity corrupted by classic heathenism, as in the Roman Catholic Church; sometimes interpenetrated by Oriental theosophy, as in the Gnostic heresies; sometimes crusted over with barbaric superstition, as in the Coptic and Abyssinian Churches: but I have never met a form of Historical Christianity that did not bear plain trace of its Author's hand.

---

* Boston, 1859, p. 100.

Nor could there be a more striking proof of █████ vitality and power. But what Christianity is █████ not been the only condition of theological █████ Apparently, no man can study and formulate █████ Records uninfluenced by his own character, █████ the spirit of his time. He interfuses into █████ part of himself. Theology is not, and cann██ impersonal, like the mathematics or the phy████ Hence it is that the historic theologies have █████ fully influenced by the men who moulded █████ the intellectual, political, and moral state of █████ in the midst of which they have been devel█████ it is that the history of doctrines has been so d█████ by individual, national, and secular peculiarit█████ words of Mr. Bernard:

"This is a process which goes on through descending ages, and i█ which every generation bears its part. It has gained accessions from al those varieties of the human mind which have been placed in contac with revealed truth, from the idiosyncracies of persons, of nations, o ages, from Fathers and Councils, from controversies and heresies, fron Hellenist, Alexandrian, and Roman forms of thought, from the mind o the East and the mind of the West, from corruptions and reformation of religion, from Italy and England, from Germany and Geneva, fron authority and inquiry, from Church and Dissent. These words and other like them represent the varying measures of apprehension, and the vary ing kinds of expression which the Gospel revelation has found amon§ men. The developments of doctrine * * thus originated wer< the joint product of the revealed truth and the condition of the min< which received it. The revealed truth was one, but the conditions of th< human mind are infinitely various; and hence an endless variety in th< developments themselves,—a variety which sometimes melts into a highe harmony, but more often jars on our ears in irreconcilable discord."*

To discuss this subject thoroughly would be a large un dertaking. I shall attempt nothing more than to stat< some of the large facts, or groups of facts, that shapec the development of primitive Christianity. A river tha

---

The Progress of Doctrine in the New Testament—Boston, 1870, pp. 34-5.

flows through a level plain takes its own cou[rse to the] sea; but the river that flows through a mount[ainous re-] gion must conform to the physical characteristi[cs of the] country. The stream of historical Christianity[, as well] as that of doctrinal development, has now flowe[d in one] direction, then in that, has been flexed here a[nd there] according as its progress was facilitated or impede[d by the] facts of history.

By the time Christianity was delivered to men, [the arms] and jurisprudence of Rome, together with the c[ulture of] Greece, had reduced the ancient world to a [condition] approaching the homogeneous. The arms had su[bdued] the nations, the jurisprudence had bound them up [into one] vast political body, and the culture had given [a certain] unity of thought, expression, and taste to th[e whole.] Partly through the shocks of war, and partly th[rough the] action of intellectual and moral forces, society h[ad to] a great degree liquified. In the midst of this [sea] of Græco-Roman civilization, lay Judea, th[e only] mass on which the Greek solvents ever acte[d; it was] disintegrated, but not dissolved. Judea sta[nds as the] first great group of facts that determined the [course and] stream of Christian thought.

II.—TWO ELEMENTS OF CIVILIZATION.

Civilization contains but two elements of the first c[lass.] One is custom, the other change; the first legality, the s[ec-] ond progress. A people must first of all be reduced to order, must be disciplined; and this must come through their subjection to a body of law. In the words of one who has discussed the subject with marked ability: "Law, rigid, definite, concise law, is the primary want of early mankind."* The object of law is to create what this writer calls a "cake of custom." The first thing to acquire, as he expresses it, is

"The legal fibre: a polity first—what sort of polity is immaterial; a law first—what kind of law is secondary; a person or set of persons to pay deference to—though who he is, or they are, by comparison scarcely signifies."†

But while civilization begins with legality, that is with rule and rules, it does not end there. Having acquired some discipline, a community must move forward. We are hardly willing to call a people who are stationary civilized. Says this author once more:

"The great difficulty which history records is not that of the first step, but that of the second step. What is most evident is not the difficulty of getting a fixed law, but getting out of a fixed law; not of cementing a cake of custom, but of breaking the cake of custom; not of making the first preservative habit, but of breaking through it, and reaching something better."‡

And once more:

"The beginning of civilization is marked by an intense legality; that legality is the very condition of its existence, the bond which ties it together; but that legality—that tendency to impose a settled customary yoke upon all men and all actions—if it goes on, kills out the very ability implanted by nature, and makes different men and different ages facsimiles of other men and other ages, as we see them so often. Progress is only possible in those happy cases where the force of legality has gone far enough to bind the nation together, but not far enough to kill out all varieties and destroy a nation's perpetual tendency to change."§

Some of the non-civilized peoples have never taken the first of these steps; others have never taken the second.

---

* Mr. Bagehot, *Physics and Politics*, N. Y., 1873, p. 21.
† *Ibid.*, p. 50.   ‡ *Ibid.*, p. 53.   § *Ibid.*, p. 64.

III.—THE LAW.

This analysis throws a flood of light upon the history of the Jewish nation. In the first place, no people, not even the Romans themselves, were ever more thoroughly subjugated to the principle of legality. But this was only after a long struggle. Moses found his countrymen stiff-necked; so did his successors in the leadership; it seemed as though the resolute, stubborn character which had been formed in the tents of the patriarchs would never bow to the legal yoke, and without the captivity in Egypt it is doubtful whether it ever would have bowed; but by and by, after frequent reverses and chastisements, the customary rule was thoroughly established. In their unyielding coherence, unfaltering devotion to their national institutions, in their obstinate refusal to succumb to external attack or internal dissolution, in their inveterate conservatism—is seen the power of their hereditary discipline. The value of legality was impressed by the history of those Jews who lapsed from the Law, especially those who followed the lead of Jeroboam. From being the most unstable, the Jews became the most stable of nations. In the words of Goethe:

"At the judgment-seat of the God of nations, it is not asked whether this is the best, the most excellent nation; but whether it lasts, whether it has continued. The Israelitish people * * possess few virtues and most of the faults of other nations; but in cohesion, steadfastness, valor, and, when all this could not serve, in obstinate toughness, it has no match. It is the most perseverant nation in the world: it is, it was, it will be, to glorify the name of Jehovah through all ages."*

Although scattered over the globe, Israel, thanks to the power of his hereditary discipline, is a nation still.

---

* *Wilhelm Meister*, Chap. XI.

IV.—THE PRIESTHOOD.

One of the most noticeable features of the Law was the minuteness and rigidity of its ritual. In this the principle of legality was firmly rooted. Over this ritual, the thoroughly organized and disciplined body known as the priesthood stood guard. The principal function of this body is thus graphically described by Dean Stanley:

"The arrangements of the Temple were, as has been truly said, not those of a cathedral or a church, but of a vast slaughter-house, combined with a banqueting-hall. Droves of oxen, sheep, and goats crowded the courts. Here were the rings to which they were fastened. There was the huge altar, towering above the people, on which the carcases were laid to be roasted. Underneath was the drain to carry off the streams of blood. Close by was the apparatus for skinning and fleecing them. Round the court were the kitchens for cooking the meat after the sacrifice was over. For that which constitutes Christian devotion, prayer, praise, commemoration, exhortation, there was not in the original Mosaic ritual any provision."*

Such, in their outward character, were the ordinances described by Paul as "fleshly," "carnal." And the regular ministers of such a worship were appropriately drawn from the sanguinary tribe of Levi. We do not need here to touch on the intrinsic meaning of the Jewish sacrifice. To quote Dean Stanley once more:

"These ideas lie unexpressed in the worship itself. All that was seen in the Mosaic system was the mechanical observance of acts which, to our mind, not only fail to carry any religious idea, but are associated with one of the coarsest of human occuptions. For this purpose, as for the defence of the shrine, not moral or intellectual qualifications were chiefly needed. The robust frame, which could endure the endless routine of the sacrifices, and carry away the bleeding remains; the quick eye and ready arm which could strike the fatal blow,—these were naturally inherent in the fierce tribe of soldier-shepherds, and these were accordingly dedicated to the Temple service."*

The priests were not the teachers or the inspirers of the

---

* *History Jewish Church*, Lecture 36.   † *Ibid.*, Lecture 36.

Jewish people. It is true that they had a teaching function, but this was of a subordinate character, mostly confined to ritualistic duties. And yet, despite the grossness and mechanical nature of its function, despite its ritualistic tendencies, the priesthood remained the center and rallying point of the nation. Nor was this so much despite its moral deficiencies as on account of them. The Jewish priesthood stood as the type of the customary or legal element in the Jewish economy.

The sacrificial system was admirably calculated to secure the principle of legality, but it contained no element of change, made no provision for new truths or inspirations. It was powerless to break the cake of custom. More than this, it was attended by one great and constant danger—the danger that threatens all religions, and especially those that abound in ceremonial elements—viz: that morality would be separated from religion, and that worship would degenerate into a set of useless forms and empty ceremonies. The Jewish religion was indeed grounded in the great truths of ethics and spirituality, of which we have so admirable a summary in the Decalogue; but the danger was, that these truths would be lost sight of in the presence of such elaborate ritualistic and casuistical arrangements—that the Jew would forget the rock from which he had been hewed, and the pit from which he had been digged.

V.—THE PROPHETS.

Hence, it is not a little remarkable that at about the time when the monarchy was established, when the nation was becoming consolidated, when the Temple took the place of the Tabernacle, when Jerusalem came to be regarded as "the place where men ought to worship," when the triumph of ritualism, owing to the final organization of the priesthood by David and Solomon, seemed complete—it is a remarkable fact, that *then* the Prophetic Order, the compensation of the priesthood and the type of religious progress, came prominently before the national mind. It is true there were earlier prophets, as Moses, but the long succession of prophets proper began with Samuel, the contemporary of Saul and David.*

The Hebrew word *nabi* is derived from the verb *naba*, which, in its religious sense, means to speak or sing under a divine afflatus or impulse; and the Greek προφήτης, employed by the Seventy to translate *nabi*, a word which has passed into all modern languages, means one who speaks for or in behalf of another. Hence the prophet was the messenger or interpreter of the Divine Will.

"Prophecy came not in old time by the will of man, but holy men of God spake as they were moved by the Holy Ghost."✝

"God at sundry times and in divers manners spake in times past unto the fathers by the prophets."‡

Here was the possibility of progress. Mr. Bagehot says:

"The Jewish nation has its type of progress in the prophets, side by side with its type of permanence in the Law and Levites. * * * All that is new comes from the prophets; all that is old is retained by the priests."§

No writer has better pointed out the influence of the two orders on the culture of the Hebrew people, than Mr. J. S. Mill. He says:

"In contrast with these nations [the Egyptian and Chinese,] let us consider the example of an opposite character afforded by another and

---

* So the Jews were accustomed to hold; see Acts iii: 24; xiii: 20; Hebs. xi: 32.
✝ II. Peter i: 21.
‡ Hebs. i: 1.
§ *Physics and Politics*, p. 63.

a comparatively insignificant Oriental people—the Jews. They too had an absolute monarchy and a hierarchy, and their organized institutions were as obviously of sacerdotal origin as those of the Hindoos. These did for them what was done for other Oriental races by their institutions—subdued them to industry and order, and gave them a national life. But neither their kings nor their priests ever obtained, as in those other countries, the exclusive moulding of their character. Their religion, which enabled persons of genius and high religious tone to be regarded and to regard themselves as inspired from heaven, gave existence to an inestimably precious unorganized institution—the Order (if it may be so termed) of Prophets. Under the protection, generally though not always effectual, of their sacred character, the Prophets were a power in the nation, often more than a match for kings and priests, and kept up, in that little corner of the earth, the antagonism of influences which is the only real security for continued progress. Religion, consequently, was not there what it has been in so many other places — a consecration of all that was once established, and a barrier against farther improvement. * * Conditions more favorable to progress could not easily exist; accordingly, the Jews, instead of being stationary like other Asiatics, were, next to the Greeks, the most progressive people of antiquity, and, jointly with them, have been the starting-point and main propelling agency of modern civilization."*

Mr. Mill even quotes the remark of the distinguished Hebrew, M. Salvador, "That the prophets were in church and state the equivalent of the modern liberty of the press," as giving "a just but not an adequate conception of the part fulfilled in national and universal history by this great element of Jewish life."

Both Mr. Bagehot and Mr. Mill take a purely rationalistic or secular view of the functions and relations of the priestly and prophetic orders. But what they say is quite as true from a religious stand-point. The priest was a born conservative, inclined to accept the situation, indisposed to either lead or favor reforms. He even acquiesced in apostasy, and sometimes ministered at altars on which "strange fire" consumed sacrifices offered to other gods.*

---

* *Representative Government*, New York, 1862, pp. 51-3.
* Ezekiel xx: 31-40.

The prophet led or inspired most of the great religious reforms. He was the Jewish preacher—the spiritual progenitor of the Christian evangelist, though speaking with an unusual authority. He more and more spiritualized the national religion, as any one can see who compares the Prophets with the Law. His moral superiority to the priest is seen in the way in which his work came to him. While the priestly office was strictly hereditary, the prophet's "call" came to shepherds, goat-herds, members of the court, and, marking its universality, even to members of the sacred tribe. And when the prophet's mantle fell on the priest, it clothed him with new dignity, power, and glory. How much superior to the priest is the prophet-priest! How much greater are Jeremiah, Ezekiel, and John the Baptist, as preachers of righteousness, than they would have been as mere sacerdotal functionaries! Holy castes and classes are always jealous of intruders, and, to secure a more complete monopoly of holy offices in their own hands, they generally insist on some difficult terms of admission. Sometimes it is nothing more than a severe and solemn service of ordination, standing at the portal of the sacerdotal life. It is, therefore, the more remarkable that, with the exception of Elisha, in the history of the prophets there is no trace of a consecrating or anointing. Perhaps this is a hint to all religious bodies belonging to the great spiritual lineage, that, if they would not have the ministry degenerate into a mechanical sacerdotalism, they must give large play to individual force and inspiration. Once more, the prophet does not attempt to supplant the priest; he recognizes his place and his functions; but, by insisting that moral duties are superior to sacrifices and ordinances, he seeks to prevent the national religion from becoming a petrifaction. How full and clear their voices ring out across the centuries!

SAMUEL.—"To obey is better than sacrifice, and to hearken than the fat of rams."*

DAVID.—"Thou desirest not sacrifice; else would I give it. Thou delightest not in burnt-offerings. The sacrifices of God are a broken spirit.   *   *   *   Sacrifice and offering Thou didst not desire. *   *   Then said I, Lo, I come. I delight to do Thy will, O my God."†

MICAH.—"Wherewith shall I come before the Lord, and bow myself before the high God? Shall I come before Him with burnt-offerings, with calves of a year old? Will the Lord be pleased with thousands of rams, or with ten thousands of rivers of oil? Shall I give my first-born for my transgression, the fruit of my body for the sin of my soul? He hath showed thee, O man, what is good ; and what doth the Lord require of thee, but to do justly, and to love mercy, and to walk humbly with thy God?"‡

ISAIAH.—"To what purpose is the multitude of your sacrifices unto me? saith the Lord: I am full of the burnt offerings of rams, and the fat of fed beasts; and I delight not in the blood of bullocks, or of lambs, or of he-goats. When ye come to appear before me, who hath required this at your hand, to tread my courts? Bring no more vain oblations: incense is an abomination unto me; the new moons and sabbaths, the calling of assemblies, I cannot away with; it is iniquity, even the solemn meeting. Your new moons and your appointed feasts my soul hateth: they are a trouble unto me; I am weary to bear them. And when ye spread forth your hands I will hide mine eyes from you; yea, when ye make many prayers I will not hear: your hands are full of blood. Wash you, make you clean; put away the evil of your doings from before mine eyes; cease to do evil; learn to do well; seek judgment, relieve the oppressed, judge the fatherless, plead for the widow. Come now, and let us reason together, saith the Lord: though your sins be as scarlet, they shall be as white as snow; though they be red like crimson, they shall be as wool."§

He has read the Old Testament to but small purpose who has not recognized these two opposing elements in Jewish life. "Compare the exaltation of moral duties in the Books of Kings with the exaltation of merely ceremonial duties in the Books of Chronicles," says Dean

---

* I Samuel xv: 22.

† Psalms li: 16, 17; xl: 6-8.

‡ Micah vi: 6-8.

§ Isaiah i: 11-18.

Stanley, "and the difference between the two elements of the sacred history is at once apparent."*

With Malachi, the messenger, the succession of goodly seers came to an end. The Levitical Institutes had now been supplemented by the Prophets; the Old Testament canon was closed; the stream of inspiration ceased, not to flow again until the opening of a new dispensation. For four hundred years the prophet disappeared from Hebrew history. From the time of his disappearance the national religion became a dead sea of stagnation and death.

"After the death of Haggai, Zechariah, and Malachi, the last of the prophets," says the Talmud, "the spirit disappeared from Israel."

"When once this vast organization, with its minuteness of ritual," says De Pressense, "ceased to be constantly vivified by the breath of prophecy often passing over it, like a Divine whirlwind, to shake its entire fabric, its tendency was to petrify into immobility."†

At the expiration of the four centuries, in the days of Herod the king, the word of God came unto John, the son of Zacharias, who began to stir the stagnant waters, in the spirit and power of Elijah. The people counted him a prophet; he was certified as a prophet and more than a prophet; and yet he was but the harbinger of one in whom the great office culminated—Jesus Christ, our Lord.

VI.—THE RABBIS.

So soon as the prophetic fires began to pale, a new life arose among the Chosen People. Immediately after the return from Babylon we meet the Synagogue and the Sanhedrim; also the doctor, scribe or rabbi. These features mark a new era in the history of Israel. A new element

---

* *Hist. Jewish Church*, Sec. XX.
† *Jesus Christ—Times, Life and Work:* London, '68, p. 62.

now enters into the national life, namely, the Rabbinical or theological. The Rabbi is the Jewish theologian; for so soon as the canon of inspiration was closed, and even before, he began his work of commenting, expounding, and summarizing. Dean Milman describes Rabbinism as that system of teaching

"Which, supplanting the original religion of the Jews, became, after the ruin of the Temple and the extinction of the public worship, a new bond of national union, the great distinctive feature in the character of modern Judaism."*

After the Captivity, Jewish institutions could never be fully restored; the change in political and social conditions, as well as the change wrought in the people themselves, made it forever impossible. But one lesson had, at last, been thoroughly inculcated—abhorrence of idolatry. The Jews now became intensely provincial. They clung all the more closely to their time-honored institutions, or what they regarded such, because they could not be fully restored. Canon Westcott has happily said:

"The very zeal with which the people sought to fulfill the Law contained the germ of that noxious growth by which it was finally overpowered."†

The Chosen People had escaped from polytheism and idolatry only to fall an easy prey to the pedant and the ritualist. Says the writer just quoted:

"Not only was the integrity of their national character endangered, but they were exposed to the subtle temptation of substituting formulas for life." ‡

Under the leadership of the Rabbi, the minutiæ of the Law usurped the place that belonged to its substance; tradition sat in the seat of Moses and the prophets; religious

---

* *History of the Jews*, vol. II, p. 415.
* *Introduction to the Study of the Gospels*, London, 1867, p. 55.
* *Ibid.* p. 55.

perspective altogether faded away; the jots and tittles of the sacred text became the objects of a superstitious solicitude, while its spirit was lost sight of altogether. "On every apostrophe in the Bible hang whole mountains of hidden sense," became an accepted Rabbinical maxim. The Jew trembled at the altar lest some trivial formality of sacrificial casuistry had been forgotten or mistaken. Conscience had become wholly artificial. "Even at every meal," says Millman, "the scrupulous conscience shuddered at the possibility, lest by some neglect or misinterpretation of the statute, it might fall into serious offence."* The Jewish Rabbi was a minister of the letter that killeth, not of the spirit that giveth life.

The essence of Rabbinism is contained in the famous precept: "Be deliberate in judgment; train up many disciples; and make a fence for the Law." The Scriptural expositions by which the early Rabbis sought to control the Jewish mind became traditional. "Tradition is the check of the Law," was a current saying. Many of these expositions were currently attributed to Moses and the early elders. The Talmud was to be read twice as much as the Bible. Scribes ranked above both kings and priests. To honor the master, that is the Rabbi, was the same thing as to honor God. Eternal gratitude was due him who had taught a single letter of the Law. "Take thy master for thy guide," said Gamaliel, "that thou mayst not fall into doubt." The Scriptures were grossly perverted, and always in the interest of Rabbinism. The Law declared, "Thou shalt not seethe the kid in his mother's milk;" hence it was held that the flesh of quadrupeds, or even poultry, should not be mixed with milk in cooking; nor might milk and meat be eaten except at considerable intervals. There was no end of similar puerility. The dying

---

*Hist. Jews, Vol. II, p. 417.

prophecy of Jacob concerning the Shiloh was rendered, "Neither the prince nor the scribe shall depart from Judah till the coming age." Perhaps it would be impossible to find such another instance of a system of law being made void by commentary and tradition. The Pharisees, who carried the logic of Rabbinism out to its final results, despised the common people, those engaged in the common pursuits of life, or, as they contemptuously called them, "the people of the land." This feeling inspired the arrogant passage found in the apocryphal book of Ecclesiasticus, in which the low estate of the laborer is contrasted with the high estate of the Rabbi:

"The wisdom of a learned man cometh by opportunity of leisure; and he that hath little business shall become wise. How can he get wisdom that holdeth the plow, and that glorieth in the goad, that driveth oxen, and is occupied in their labors, and whose talk is of bullocks? He giveth his mind to make furrows; and is diligent to give the kine fodder." In the same way the carpenter and work-master, they that cut and grave seals, the smith and the potter, are said "to trust in their hands: and every one is wise in his work, "Without these cannot a city be inhabited: and they shall not dwell where they will, nor go up and down. They shall not be sought for in public council, nor sit high in the congregation: they shall not sit on the judges' seat, nor understand the sentence of judgment: they cannot declare justice and judgment; and they shall not be found where parables are spoken."

On the other hand:

"He that giveth his mind to the Law of the Most High," that is the Rabbi, and "is occupied in the meditation thereof, will seek out the wisdom of all the ancient, and be occupied in prophecies. He will keep the sayings of the renowned men: and where subtil parables are, he will be there also. He will seek out the secrets of grave sentences, and be conversant in dark parables. He shall serve among great men, and appear before princes."* And much more to the same effect.

Rabbinism was wrought out into a fully elaborated system, both doctrinal and ecclesiastical. It had its elderships, schools, synagogues, and councils. It could not

---

* Ecclesiasticus, Chaps. xxxviii, ix.

fail to engender the most intense pride and arrogance. In entire forgetfulness of the grandest oracles of the Old Testament, the Rabbi proclaimed:

"All Israel has part in the world to come; each Israelite is worth more before God than all the people who have been or shall be."

"We have Abraham to our father."

This was complacently assuming that salvation came by hereditary descent.

The Rabbi was not a priest, and much less a prophet; but he did his work more effectually than either. From the close of the prophetic succession, he is the foremost character among his people. As the priest emphasized sacrifice and oblation, as the prophet emphasized justice, mercy, and faith, so the Rabbi emphasized doctrinal soundness. The man who forgot a point of doctrine was on the way to ruin. Nor must we overlook the fact that the Rabbi entirely subverted the old Law, at least in its bolder and grander features, and substituted a new law—a law of his own making—in its place. Christ repeatedly charged him with making void the Law of God by his traditions. At the same time, however, he was a thoroughgoing conservative. The new departure was made so slowly, it proceeded by such short stages, the heart of the Old Testament was so imperceptibly eaten out, that it is hardly possible the Rabbi was aware of the change. Rabbinism was the final triumph of the letter over the spirit, of tradition and authority over inspiration and life. The principle of progress ceased altogether to play in Jewish history, and the principle of legality firmly bound the nation. In the history of Rabbinism we can clearly discern the great truth, that the ultra conservative is the very man who loses everything belonging to the past that is worth preserving. Very naturally, the work of the Rabbi mingled with that of the priest; the Rabbinical and sacerdotal elements blended in the national culture; so that such another nation of ritualists and pedants as the Jews became was never seen. How effectually the souls of men were ensnared in the toils of Rabbinism, can be learned from the New Testament. In the time of Christ men were esteemed pious in the ratio of the width of their phylacteries and the ostentation of their prayers. The Scribes sat in Moses's seat, teaching with authority. Legalism reigned supreme on the throne of religion. A wicked and adulterous generation, destitute of spiritual apperception, clamored for "a sign." Israel had become a moral petrifaction. Even the glorious Messianic predictions, so long the hope and solace of the nation, were perverted. So gross and sensual had the nation become, that they would have none but a temporal Messiah. Accordingly, they turned away from Him of whom Moses in the Law and the Prophets did write, not knowing the day of their visitation.

VII.—HELLENISM.

Only one stroke of lighter color can the faithful artist lay upon the canvas. From the day that the conquests of Alexander extended the Grecian name and influence over the East, the Jew, in common with the other Orientals, felt the spell of the Hellenic genius. The Grecian solvents disintegrated and dissolved almost everything that they came into contact with, but they never dissolved Judaism. At the same time, however, large numbers of Jews were profoundly influenced by the Grecian culture and language.

It must be remembered that, at this time, the Jewish nation was divided into two great classes—Palestinian

Jews and Jews of the Dispersion (Διασπορά). Originally these were mere geographical descriptions. The Palestinian Jews were those who lived in Palestine—the proper home of the race; the dispersed or scattered Jews were the "strangers" in foreign countries. Collectively, these suggested the address to James's Epistle, "To the twelve tribes which are scattered abroad [or in the dispersion], Greeting."* They may be divided into several minor groups: First, the "captivity," ("the dispersed among the Babylonians" of Josephus,) found in Assyria, Media, Babylonia, and Persia. Second, the Egyptian colony, dating from the founding of Alexandria. Third, the "dispersed" of Syria and Asia Minor, (the latter of which suggested the address of Peter, "'To the strangers scattered throughout Pontius, Galatia," etc.) Fourth, the Jews of Greece and Macedonia, (the "dispersed among the Greeks," not "Gentiles," of John vii: 35.) Last of all, the Roman Jews, (the "strangers of Rome," of Acts ii: 10,) whose settlement in Italy dates from the time of Pompey.

The description of Jewish religion given above is intended for the Palestinian Jews chiefly. They clung to the traditional faith and culture with desperate tenacity. They spoke the Aremæan language, "the sacred tongue of Palestine;" not the old Hebrew of their fathers, but a kindred dialect; not the language of Moses and David, but of Ezra and Nehemiah. Originally a geographical description, the expression "Palestinian Jew" or "Hebrew" came to denote a certain habit of mind or tone of thought —a certain relation to the old faith, in a word. Living remote from the Temple, which they visited but rarely, removed, in a degree, from the disciplinary traditions of the nation, and surrounded by Gentile influences, the Jews of

---

* James i: 1.

the Dispersion naturally lacked somewhat of the narrowness and rigidity that belonged to their Palestinian brethren, and became more roomy and liberal in their views. Notably was this true of those who came under the spell of the Greek genius. Alexandria was their capital, in an intellectual and theological sense; Greek was their literary language; and they read the Scriptures in the Version of the Seventy. In the words of Dean Howson:

> "The division went deeper than mere superficial diversity of speech. It was not only a division, like the modern one of German and Spanish Jews, where those who hold substantially the same doctrines have been accidentally led to speak different languages. But there was a diversity of religious views and opinions."*

After saying that such foreign elements as were found in the Palestinian culture were rather Oriental or Babylonian than Greek, the Dean goes on to say:

> "The work of the learned Hellenists may be briefly described as this,—to accommodate Jewish doctrines to the mind of the Greeks, and to make the Greek language express the mind of the Jews. The Hebrew principles were disengaged as much as possible from local and national conditions, and presented in a form adapted to the Hellenic world. All this was hateful to the zealous Aramæans. The men of the East rose up against those of the West. The Greek learning was not more repugnant to the Roman Cato, than it was to the strict Hebrews. They had a saying, 'Cursed be he who teacheth his son the learning of the Greeks.' We could imagine them using the words of the prophet Joel (iii: 6), 'The children of Judah and the children of Jerusalem have ye sold unto the Grecians, that ye might remove them from their border:' and we cannot be surprised that, even in the deep peace and charity of the Church's earliest days, this inveterate division reappeared, and that 'when the number of the disciples was multiplied there arose a murmuring of the Grecians against the Hebrews.' "†

What has now been said prepares the way for some definitions of New Testament terms, that must never be lost sight of.

---

* Life and Epistles of St. Paul, vol. I, p. 36.
† *Ibid.* vol. i, pp. 36, 7.

HELLENISM. 27

The term *Jew* means a subject of the Kingdom of Judah, a descendant of Jacob, and includes all the members of the Theocracy without reference to country or language. It is a national designation.

Hebrew has a double meaning. Sometimes it means simply a Jew; sometimes a Palestinian Jew—a Jew of orthodox theology. An example of this second use is found in Acts vi: 1, as will be shown in Part Second.

Grecian means a Grecian or Hellenistic Jew, often called simply a Hellenist. Examples are found in Acts vi: 1, and ix: 29.

Greek means, first, a Greek, a man whose proper country is Greece; second, a Pagan or a Gentile of any nationality. Examples of the first use are Joel iii: 6; Acts xi: 20, (both of which, in the common version, erroneously read "Grecians"), and Acts xviii: 17; examples of the second use, chaps. xiv: 1, and xvi: 1, of the same book.

It remains to add, the terms "Aramæan" and "Hellenistic," "Hebrew," and "Grecian," came to be used in a sense almost wholly conventional. "Grecian" synagogues were numerous in Jerusalem*—that is, synagogues where the "Grecian" tone of religious thought prevailed; founded and supported, of course, by Jews of the Dispersion who had come up to the Holy City to reside. "Grecians" living in Jerusalem were early brought into the Church.† Also "Hebrew" Jews were scattered among their Hellenistic countrymen in many of the places where the latter were found, and so formed a sort of dispersion themselves. But the old geographical meaning of "Hebrew" and "Greek" did not wholly fade out. Jews of the Dispersion, even Hellenistic Jews, were sometimes Palestinian in theology. As Dean Howson puts it, all

---

* Acts vi: 9. † Acts vi: 1.

Hellenists were not Hellenizers. Saul of Tarsus and his family are notable examples of this exceptional class. More than once Paul declared himself "a Pharisee" and "the son of a Pharisee," * and when he called himself "a Hebrew of the Hebrews," as he twice did,† he probably means, not that he was Hebrew in nationality, but in doctrine.

I have been particular to state these facts because a clear perception of them is the key to many a New Testament problem; and because, also, they reveal an important element in the later Jewish culture. It is clear that the influence of the Greek mind over the Hebrew mind was, to give the latter a broader range, a freer movement, and a spirit of catholicity. Educated as the Jew had been, Grecian rationalism was far better for his soul than Palestinian Rabbinism.

VIII —RECAPITULATION.

It has now been shown : (1) What are the conditions of a growth and what are their power; (2) That legality and progress are the two main elements in civilization; That Judaism has its principle of legality and permanence (3) in its Law and (4) its Priesthood; and (5) its element of progress in the Prophetic Order. It has also been shown (6) What was the nature and what the power of Rabbinism; and (7) How the Jewish lump was partially leavened by the spirit of Hellenism.

---

* Acts xxiii: 6; Phil. iii: 5.
† II. Cor. xi: 22; Phil. iii: 5.

But this First Part is only introductory to the Second. We are now to witness the introduction of the Gospel—the Spirit and the Truth, into this mass of legalism, tradition, carnal ordinances, and sacerdotalism.

PART SECOND.

THE JEWISH-CHRISTIAN CHURCH.

I.—INTRODUCTION.

The wide field of Christian Dogmatics is divided into several departments. They are Theology Proper, the Doctrine of God, His Being and Attributes; Christology, the Doctrine of Christ, His Person and Nature; Anthropology, the Doctrine of Man, including Sin and Grace; Soteriology, the Doctrine of Christ as a Saviour; Eschatology, the Doctrine of the Future State of the Soul, including the Second Advent of Christ and the Judgment; Ecclesiology, the Doctrine of the Church, its Object, Organization, and Prerogatives. It has been pointed out by numerous writers, and notably by Kliefoth, that these different departments of dogmatics have been cultivated in a given historical order and by different sections of the Church Universal. "To the Greek mind and the Greek Church was assigned," he says, "the task of elaborating the doctrine of the Bible concerning God, *i. e.*, the doctrines of the Trinity and Person of Christ; to the Latin Church the doctrines concerning Man, that is, of Sin and Grace; to the German Church, Soteriology, or the doctrine of Justification." Kliefoth further says: "Ecclesiology is reserved for the future, as the doctrine concerning the Church has not been settled by Œcumenical authority, as have been the doctrines of Theology and Anthropology, and that of Justification at least for the Protestant world."* It will be seen that this wide generalization, which is as just as it is comprehensive, does not include the Jewish-Christian Church. Nor did this Church at any time develop a single article of what is called the Catholic Christian Faith. Judea made no contributions to positive dogmatics. But it must not therefore be inferred that the Jewish mind had no influence on theological development. Its influence can be traced in three distinct particulars, two of them negative, one positive, and all well worthy of study.

In the first place, Judea is historically the point of departure for all theological speculation. To the Jews were committed the earlier Oracles of God; their language was the vehicle of the Old Testament Revelation; the events of their history, the names of their rivers, plains, and mountains passed into the spiritual vocabulary of Christendom.† Their highest spiritual aspirations have been re-

---

* See Hodge's *Systematic Theology*, vol. i, p. 32; also Shedd's *Hist. Doctrine*, vol. i. pp. 33, 4 and 40, 41.

† "Not only has the long course of ages invested the prospects and scenes of the Holy Land with poetical and moral associations, but these scenes lend themselves to such parabolical adaptation with singular facility. Far more closely as in some respects the Greek and Italian geography intertwines itself with the history and religion of the two countries; yet when we take the proverbs, the apologues, the types furnished even by Parnassus and Helicon, the Capitol and the Rubicon, they bear no comparison with the appropriateness of the corresponding figures and phrases borrowed from Arabian and Syrian topography, even irrespectively of the wider diffusion given them by our greater familiarity with the Scriptures. The passage of the Red Sea — the wilderness of life—the Rock of Ages — Mount Sinai and its terrors— the view from Pisgah—the passage of the Jordan—the rock of Zion, and the fountain of Siloa—the lake of Gennesareth, with its storms, its waves, and its fishermen, are well-known instances in which the local features of the Holy Land have naturally become the household imagery of Christendom.—Dean Stanley, *Sinai and Palestine*, Preface, pp. 22, 3.

produced under a better economy than their own. The "goodly seers" who foretold the coming glory were of their race On the human side, Christ was a Jew; the first evangelists of the new faith were Jews; the New Testament was written by Jews, and although its language is Greek, its imagery is mostly Jewish. The four great types of New Testament doctrine—types differing somewhat in particulars, but blending in a higher unity—are the forms in which four Jews apprehended Christ's religion. More than all, Christianity was an evolution from the Jewish faith and worship. Accordingly, Judea is the historical background of Christianity, and, therefore, of Christian theology.

In the second place, the Jews originated one of the historical conceptions of Christianity; the Jewish mind was the first to conceive it under what we may call the Levitical aspect. There are two antagonistical conceptions of the Gospel—one moral or spiritual, paying attention to the reason and intent of the Scripture ; the other legal, limited by the externality of the statute. As a natural result of his traditional discipline, the Jewish disciple generally tended to the second. He did not tend to resolve Christianity into a body of speculative divinity, like the Greek, or to build up a hierarchical system out of its ecclesiastical elements, like the Roman; but he treated the Gospel as a second Law; he regarded the New Testament as an enlarged and amplified Book of Leviticus. He failed to distinguish between the works of the Law and free grace, between the letter and the spirit, and employed his Rabbinical methods upon the New Scriptures as he had already employed them on the Old. It would be too much to say, the temper of mind that naturally contemplates the Scriptures under the Levitical aspect was confined to the Jew; it belongs to other races, and is found among all races. No doubt it would have shown itself somewhere else if not among the Jewish Christians; but we must remember that it first appeared among them, and that it is peculiarly their own.

In the third place, the first great heresy within the Church was a Jewish heresy. It was a peculiar view of the Person and Work of Christ, and flowed as naturally from the Jewish habit of conceiving the Gospel under a legal aspect as that habit itself resulted from the traditionary Jewish discipline. Greece and Rome contributed directly to the substance of theology, and therefore conditioned it positively; Judea made no positive contribution, and conditioned it only negatively. What Judea really did, will be seen when we trace in outline the history of the Jewish-Christian Church.

II.—BEFORE PENTECOST.

Jesus declared, "I am not sent but unto the lost sheep of the house of Israel;"* and when He sent out the Twelve on their first mission, He instructed them to confine their labors to the same scattered flock.† He was not indifferent to the Gentile peoples; He fully intended finally to gather into the one fold all the sheep, of whatever flock, that would hear His voice; but His personal efforts and the immediate results of those efforts were almost wholly limited to the children of Abraham. On a few occasions He came in contact with Gentiles and Samaritans, and in several such cases He found a singular openness to the truth;‡ but He was not thereby diverted from his imme-

---

*Matthew xv: 24. † *Ibid.* x: 5, 6.
‡ Matthew viii: 5-13; xv: 21-28; John iv.

diate and especial work. He consorted with Jews, wrought miracles for the benefit of Jews, taught Jews; and the group of disciples that gathered about Him, including the Apostles, were, without exception, Jews. The five hundred brethren who, according to Paul,[*] were witnesses of his resurrection, were all Jews; and so were the hundred and twenty who, in Jerusalem, waited with one accord for the fulfillment of His last promise. All these are very simple, well-known facts; but their important bearing on subsequent history is not always understood.

The career of Jesus culminated, as had been predicted, in Jerusalem. He had made some disciples in the Holy City and its immediate neighborhood, but most of His company came from the provinces. The fact that His followers were called "Galileans" shows where His greatest influence had been felt, and the most devoted of His northern converts followed Him to the close of His life. How many disciples He made altogether it is impossible to tell; but we have good reason to conclude that it was a small number. What had become of those who are not found in Jerusalem during the ten days that elapsed between their Master's ascension and the succeeding Pentecost? No doubt some had lost their faith and love; but it is reasonable to suppose that there were others who remained faithful at their homes, scattered through Galilee and Judea. These scattered disciples disappeared from history; the Acts deals only with the little community of one hundred and twenty in Jerusalem—the nucleus of the Christian Church. What, then, was the mental and spiritual state of this community—what their impressions, hopes, and feelings—what their religious consciousness, before the day of Pentecost had fully come? Especially, what was their view of the new Teacher, and of their own

---

[*] I Corinthians xv: 6.

relations to the Jews and the Gentiles? The history of the early Church can never be understood until these questions are resolved, and to them I now address myself.

In the first book of the Bible the history of the Fall is accompanied by a promised restoration. Vague and general at first, this promise finally centers in a Person— the Messiah, or the Anointed One—who was to appear in "the fullness of time." For centuries this Person was the subject of prophecy. As the prophetic delineation of His character and work became clearer and clearer, the line of descent in which He was to appear became narrower and narrower; and the canon of prophecy did not close until his nation, tribe, and family had been designated, the place of His birth foretold, and the time and circumstances of His appearance approximately settled. The following passages make all these points clear:

"I will put enmity between thee and the woman, and between thy seed and her seed; it shall bruise thy head, and thou shalt bruise his heel."*

"Blessed be the Lord God of Shem."†

"And in thee [Abraham] shall all families of the earth be blessed."‡

"In Isaac shall thy seed be called."§

"Abraham shall surely become a great and mighty nation, and all the nations of the earth shall be blessed in him."∥

"The sceptre shall not depart from Judah, nor a lawgiver from between his feet, until Shiloh come; and unto Him shall the gathering of the people be."¶

"And there shall come forth a rod out of the stem of Jesse, and a branch shall grow out of his roots."**

"But thou, Bethlehem Ephratah, though thou be little among the thousands of Judah, yet out of thee shall He come forth unto me that is to be ruler in Israel."††

"The glory of this latter house shall be greater than of the former, saith the Lord of Hosts; and in this place will I give peace, saith the Lord of Hosts."‡‡

---

* Genesis iii: 15. § *Ibid.* xxi: 12. ** Isaiah xi: 1.
† *Ibid.* ix: 26. ∥ *Ibid.* xxiii: 18. †† Micah v: 2.
‡ *Ibid.* xii: 3. ¶ *Ibid.* xlix: 10. ‡‡ Haggai ii: 9.

These prophecies, with the others of similar import, made a deep impression on the Jewish mind. Long before the Christian Era dawned, the whole nation confidently expected and ardently desired the coming of the Messiah. There was, however, a skeptical class, made up chiefly of Jews who had become infected with foreign modes of thought, who did not entertain this expectation and hope; but these were the few exceptions to an almost universal rule. It was this pervading feeling that led the Jews in thousands to the banks of the Jordan, "musing in their hearts" whether John the Baptist "were the Christ or not;"* that prompted John himself to ask of Jesus, "Art thou He that should come, or do we look for another?"† and that caused the multitude to inquire, "When Christ cometh, will He do more miracles than these which this man hath done?"‡ It was the same feeling that made the Jews a constant prey to the false Messiahs, like Simon and Theudas, of whom there were so many in their later history. But perhaps the most striking proof of the strength of the Messianic hope is furnished by the fact that the Gentiles of the East—generally so hostile to Jewish ideas and feelings—came largely to share it with the Chosen People. Evidence of this is found in the well-known passages in Tacitus and Suetonius:

"There was a general belief, based on the ancient books of the Priests, that at that very time the East would become strong, and that those arising in Judea would obtain the empire of the world."§

"An old and firmly-fixed belief had spread over the entire East that, according to the fates, the Jews would at that time obtain universal empire."‖

But what sort of person did the Jews expect their Mes-

---

* Luke iii: 15.
† Matthew xi: 3.
‡ John vii: 31.
§ Hist. cap. xiii.
‖ In Vespas. iv.

siah to be, and what were their notions of His work? In other words, how did they construe the Messianic predictions of their prophets? In reply, it must be said that different individuals reached different conclusions; and when we remember the difficulties that beset the question, it must be confessed that there was nothing strange in this. It must not be forgotten that the interpretation of prophecy, especially in its minor features, is never easy until history has furnished the key. For the Jew to believe in a Messiah was one thing; for him fully to represent the Messiah, or *a* Messiah, in his own mind, was quite another thing. Besides, no one passage or book of the Old Testament gives a complete view of the person and work of the Messiah; and it is only by combining a great number of scattered descriptions and allusions— only by blending a mass of details into a synthesis—that a complete and harmonious conception can be formed. What is more, the prophets represent the Messiah under a variety of images. Moses speaks of Him as a prophet:

"The Lord thy God will raise up unto thee a Prophet from the midst of thee, of thy brethren, like unto me."*

David contemplates Him under the type of a king:

"Yet have I set my King upon my holy hill of Zion."†

He is described as the Son of God:

"Thou art my Son; this day have I begotten Thee."‡

And also the Son of Man:

"Behold, one like the Son of Man came with the clouds of heaven, and came to the Ancient of Days, and they brought him near before him. And there was given him dominion, and glory, and a kingdom, that all people, nations, and languages should serve him." §

He is represented under a variety of other aspects: He

---

* Deuteronomy xviii: 15. ‡ Psalms ii: 7.
† Psalms ii: 6. § Daniel vii: 13.

is a Conqueror and a Judge; the Counselor, the Redeemer, and the Prince of Peace; He is a suffering Saviour, "a Man of Sorrows, and acquainted with grief."*

These various representations of the Christ, seemingly contradictory, do not exclude each other. The intelligent Christian can gather the *disjecta membra* into one harmonious form; he has no difficulty in blending all the colors into one beautiful picture. But then, in interpreting the Christ of prophecy, he calls to his aid the Christ of history. Considering all the difficulties, we need not be surprised that the common Jew never formed a complete and luminous conception of the Restorer, whose coming he anticipated with such ardent hope. What was more natural than that different individuals, in forming their subjective Messiahs, should be influenced by their own culture, tone, and aspirations? Such was indeed the case. No universal conception, at once full and unvarying, is found in the Jewish literature. Sometimes the Messiah is contemplated from a point of view more gross and material, sometimes from one more pure and spiritual. Towards the last, however, the great mass of Jews came to view Him under one aspect. The later history of the nation was full of disaster and suffering; the Chosen People was despoiled by the Greek and trodden under foot by the Roman. Very naturally, among a people so patriotic, the desire for civil and religious liberty became an intense national aspiration. In bitterness of soul the people cried, "Let God arise, let His enemies be scattered."† Very naturally, the common Jew longed for a military leader who could restore his lost independence; and, just as naturally, he was led to interpret the prophecies in the light of this feeling. As a consequence, the royal or Davidic type

---

* Isaiah ix: 6, 7; liii: 3.
† Psalms lxviii: 1.

of the Messiah more and more excluded the prophetic or Mosaic type; and the Messiah of the popular heart became a conqueror, like Judas Maccabeus—a Son of David, who would break the bonds of the oppressor and let the oppressed go free. Around this central idea were grouped the different elements of temporal power and royal pomp. Still it would be an exaggeration to say this ideal Messiah was nothing more than a vulgar conqueror; he was not wholly stripped of the loftier attributes with which the prophets clothed Him; but he was a political and military, rather than a spiritual prince. It does not appear that, at the last, he was thought of as a divine personage at all. His kingdom would be of the earth; he would restore the theocracy, not usher in a better dispensation. His only beatitude was, "Blessed is he that shall eat bread in the kingdom of God."*

But oppression and suffering had not carnalized and stupefied all Jewish hearts. Hence this material view of the Messiah did not universally obtain. Some minds represented Him under the more spiritual types. While calamity carnalized some, it purified others. There was a class who, like Simeon, waited for "the consolation of Israel," whose eyes desired to see the salvation of God; like Anna, who looked for redemption in Jerusalem.† But these were few in number; the great body of the nation had so lost the power of spiritual perception that they were incapable of interpreting those prophecies which, next to the traditional discipline, was the strongest bond of their union and the surest pledge of their national life. ‡

---

*Luke xiv: 15.

† *Ibid.* ii: 25-38.

‡ Westcott gives a valuable discussion of the "Jewish doctrine of the Messiah," in his "Introduction to the Study of the Gospels." After tracing the idea through the Jewish literature, he says:

On one point touching the reign of the Messiah, Jewish ideas appear to have been especially dim, confused, and wavering. The Jew read in Isaiah:

"And it shall come to pass in the last days that the mountain of the Lord's house shall be established in the top of the mountains, and shall be exalted above the hills, and all nations shall flow unto it. And many people shall go and say, Come ye, and let us go up to the mountain of the Lord, to the house of the God of Jacob; and He will teach us of His ways, and we will walk in His paths; for out of Zion shall go forth the law, and the word of the Lord from Jerusalem."*

He read in the Psalms:

"Ask of me, and I shall give thee the heathen for thine inheritance, and the uttermost parts of the earth for thy possession."†

But how did the Jew construe these Scriptures? How did he expect the promises to be fulfilled? It is not likely that the great mass of Jews ever attempted to work out, in their own minds, the future relations of the Gentiles to the Chosen People and to the Messiah. So far as they were concerned, the prophecies relating to the nations lay uninterpreted and dead in the scrolls of the Old Testament. Some of the Rabbis appear to have taught that the Gentiles would be destroyed. The current view ran about as follows: The highest earthly destiny that the Jew assigned to the Gentile, was his conversion to Judaism; his admission, through obedience to the Law, to the pale of the Jewish Church. Here he was a "proselyte," a "stranger within the gates" of the Peculiar People. Even

---

"The first thing which must strike any one who has observed the manifold sources from which the several traits of Messiah's person have been drawn, is the fragmentariness of the special conceptions formed of him. Most of the separate elements of which the whole truth consisted were known, but they were kept distinct. One feature was taken for the complete image; and the only temper which excluded all error was that of simple and devout expectation."—p. 143.

* Isaiah ii: 2, 3.
† Psalms ii: 8.

then his position was inferior and in most respects wretched: the child of Abraham by naturalization never could be equal to the child by blood. In the words of a great scholar:

"The Jews, particularly in ancient times, never thought of spreading their religion. Their religion was to them a treasure, a privilege, a blessing, something to distinguish them, as the chosen people of God, from all the rest of the world. A Jew must be of the seed of Abraham; and when in later times, owing chiefly to political circumstances, the Jews had to admit strangers to some of the privileges of their theocracy, they looked upon them, not as souls that had been gained, saved, born again into a new brotherhood, but as strangers, as proselytes; which means men who have come to them as aliens—not to be trusted, as their saying was, until the twenty-fourth generation."*

It is not likely that the practical difference between the Jew by birth and the Jew by proselytism, was as distinct as the theological difference; but still it was a distinction that time only could wear out. Now, the Jewish opinion most favorable to the Gentiles appears to have been that, by and by, the latter would be proselyted. Thus, the place of the Jewish tent would be enlarged, the curtains of their habitations would be stretched forth—they would lengthen their cords and strengthen their stakes; the coming of the Messiah would be coincident with this great enlargement of Judaism; the nations would pass over the middle wall of partition; the old distinction between the Jew and the proselyte would become dim, or even effaced, in the grand flowing together: but that the National Church would be unfolded into a Universal Church, into which no one entered as a Jew or a Gentile, that the legal piety would make room for a worship in spirit and in truth, was a thought that never dawned on the common Jewish mind.

Christ gathered His disciples from the more teachable of

---

* Max Muller, *Lect. on Missions.*

His countrymen with whom he came into close contact. Every one that was of the truth heard His voice and followed Him.* And yet His leading disciples shared the prevailing legal piety; and the basis of their Messianic faith was the prevalent temporal ideal, though the Messiah of their minds may have been invested with more of the higher prophetic attributes. How much did Christ's instruction and intercourse do for these disciples? First of all, they became convinced before His death that He was the Messiah, though they were far from understanding the character of His reign until some time afterwards. The mother of two chief Apostles, with their full concurrence and probably at their instigation, asked that one of her sons might sit on His right hand and the other on His left, in His kingdom.† So ingrained in their minds was the political conception of the Messiah and the Levitical conception of religion, that constant corrections of their coarse ideas produced little impression. Rightly considered, Christ's frequent question, "Do ye not *yet* understand?" is one of the most pathetic of his laments. When under the shadow of the cross, their faith in Him, as the Messiah, again wavered; two of them said, "We *trusted* that it had been He which should have redeemed Israel."‡ This is the language of a broken trust, and the feeling that prompted it was no doubt shared to a great extent by all the members of the stricken flock. But His resurrection and fresh expositions of the Prophets remove their last lingering doubts; they are converted; Jesus is, at last, the Messiah of His people. Still, even after the resurrection the temporal conception of His mission remains, as is shown by the question, "Lord wilt thou at this time re-

---

* John, xviii: 37.
† Matt. xx: 20-8; Mark x: 35-45.
‡ Luke xxiv: 21.

store again the kingdom to Israel?"* His ascension puts an end to their expectations of an immediate Messianic reign on earth; they look, however, for His speedy return " in like manner as they have seen Him go into heaven;"† but John and James no longer ask or desire to sit on either hand of a temporal prince. The realization of any materialistic ideas that linger in their minds, is postponed to the millennial reign. In the mean time, to them the Kingdom of God is one of spirit, the reign of Christ is over the soul. But during the days that they wait in Jerusalem, in prayer and supplication for the endowment of the Spirit, what is their view of the Gentile world? Their Lord has told them that repentance and remission of sins are to be preached in His name among all nations, beginning at Jerusalem:‡ they have received the great commission. But how do they regard the promise and the commission? what effect has it produced on their minds? The historian has not told us, and we are left to inference. But the data are so certain that there is small room for mistake. Their condition of mind is ecstacy, and it is not probable that they ponder the far-reaching terms of their Lord's last injunction. But in so far as they construe the command at all, it means little if any more to their minds than the prophecies had meant; the Gentiles are to be converted— they have never doubted that; but they are still to approach the Messiah by the Jewish gate. Whatever rights and blessings belong henceforth to the Jew, belong also to the Gentile; but between the latter and participation stands the Mosaic law as well as the commands of Christ. We need not suppose that their point of view is wholly Jewish. Perhaps their interest in the Gentiles has been quickened; perhaps the Messiah stands in a more interest-

---

* Acts i: 6. † *Ibid.* i: 11. ‡ Luke xxiv: 47.

ing relation to the nations than they had thought; perhaps their hearts begin to throb with the spirit of proselytism, which, under the divine guidance, is destined to become the spirit of evangelization: but that they are yet far from understanding both the prophecies and the commission, no student of the New Testament would think of denying. So long a time does it take to unfold the Christian flower from the dry old Jewish bud ! for the tender plant to grow out of the dry ground!

Christ told his Apostles that they should be his " witnesses both in Jerusalem, and in all Judea, and in Samaria, and unto the uttermost part of the earth;"* thus describing the concentric circles by which His religion should be propagated. We are now to move from the centre of these circles outward. We must trace the history of the Church through several series of events, watching all the time the unfolding of the Christian consciousness.

[De Pressense gives this animated account of the Jewish consciousness at the Advent :

"The age which saw the birth of Messiah was quivering with mysterious expectation. The often-quoted words of Suetonius about the universal ruler who was to come from the East, are only an echo of the feverish hopes of the Jews. But closely regarded, these hopes were then more imbued than ever with a political and theocratic character. The materialistic tendency which we have pointed out in the apocryphal books, reached its culminating point precisely on the eve of the great event which was to give them the most signal contradiction. We find it faithfully expressed in the various passages of the Gospels, which bring before us the contemporaries of Christ; it is fully displayed in the Targums, in the oldest portions of the Talmud, and above all, in the great apocalypses like the book of Enoch and the fourth book of Esdras. The expected Messiah is to be a mighty king, the descendant of David.† The town of Bethlehem is at once pointed out as his birth-place by the doctors whom Herod consults,‡ and who are the faithful echo of the Targums of the period. Great sorrows are to precede the advent of the Deliverer; he will have Elias or one of the prophets as his immediate fore-

---

* Acts i: 8.   † Mark xii: 35.   ‡ Matt. ii: 5.

runner.* He is often represented under the image of a new Moses; he is to be the prophet like the prophet of Sinai, whose appearance is predicted in Deuteronomy; and miracles are looked for from him, similar to those in the desert.+ His first work will be to restore the national glory of the Jews, to reconquer the sacred soil of Palestine, and to restore the Kingdom to Israel, after having purified the people of God by repentance.‡ Such are the essential features of the picture. They are reproduced in the Targums of the time. These also ascribe to Messiah descent from David, birth at Bethlehem, a renovating influence upon the people and the deliverance of the ten tribes.§ They add that Messiah will engage in a supreme conflict with the power of evil, symbolized by the mysterious names of Gog and Magog. ‖

The Rabbis place in the second line, and as it were in the perspective of the picture, all their apocalyptic imaginations. They make the great crisis which is to precede the end of the world coincide with the era of the Messiah; sometimes they attribute to Him the resurrection of the dead and the last judgment; sometimes they make his reign the precursor of the final scenes in which God will enact the principal part. They hesitate between a general resurrection and a resurrection of the just alone.¶ But they are unanimous in seeing in the future only a brilliant triumph of Judaism, in which the nations may no doubt participate, but subordinately, and as it were in the train of the sons of Abraham. 'How beautiful is Messiah the King,' we read in Targum of a later date which is, however, a faithful echo of Pharisaic tradition; 'He has girded his loins; He has set the battle in array against His enemies; He has reddened the mountains with the blood of his adversaries.'** The Pharisees take literally the image of a new temple and a new Jerusalem. They extol the glory of Messiah, but wherever there is an apparent ascription to Him of pre-existence and of Deity, we may be convinced there has been some Christian interpolation, or, as in the fourth book of Esdras, the trace of the indirect influence of primitive Christianity. The idea of a suffering Messiah is in flagrant contradiction with their system. The possibility of suffering is only admitted with reference to a second Messiah, who appears in some of their wildest traditions, and who is to devote himself for the deliverance of the ten tribes.++—*Jesus Christ, His Times, Life and Work*, pp. 97-8.]

---

* Mark ix: 11; vi: 15; John i: 21.
+ John vi: 31.
‡ Acts i: 6.
§ Targum, Jonathan on Micah, v: 2.
‖ Gfrœrer II, p. 215.
¶ *Ibid.* II, p. 232.
** *Ibid.* p. 246.
++ "Morietur hic Messias." Gfrœrer II, pp. 259-61.

III.—JERUSALEM AND JUDEA.

Only three of the many phases of the Pentecost bear on the present inquiry.

First, Pentecost greatly increased the number of the disciples. There were added to the one hundred and twenty about three thousand souls.* The work of previous preparation, the demonstrative manifestations of the Divine Spirit, together with the fervency and power of the Apostles' preaching, all contributed to this grand result. Nor did the ingathering stop here. Conversions were made continually; "The Lord added to the Church daily such as should be saved;"† and soon the number of disciples was swollen to many thousands. It may be said here, as on a later occasion, "So mightily grew the word of the Lord and prevailed."‡

Second, we must inquire what effect the Pentecost produced on the old disciples' conception of the Gospel, so far as the relations of the old faith to the new are concerned. The endowment of the Spirit has dispelled some of the clouds previously hanging about their minds; somewhat of the old grossness has been purged away. They stand upon the top of a loftier ecstacy. Still none of them see the final bearings of Christ's mission. Few, if any, have carefully considered the question, What is the relation of the new faith to the old, of the Gospel to the Law? Few, if any, are aware that they have taken a step which logically leads to their separation from the old communion. They see in Christianity "the fulfillment" of the Law, but not its passing away; and it has not occurred to them that they are the less Jews because they have become disciples of Jesus. The great body of the new converts,

---

*Acts ii: 41.   † *Ibid.* ii: 47.   ‡ *Ibid.* xix: 20.

and perhaps all, share the same feeling. Had they understood what conversion to Christ really involved, it is impossible to say what would have been their action. It is proper to observe that our Lord never put needless difficulties in His own way. He never said the forms of the old worship would become obsolete at a given time, nor did He ever, either before or after His ascension, say, in plain, literal words that the old dispensation had come to an end. He never issued a proclamation commanding his followers to abandon the courts of the Temple, or to refrain from participation in the ancient rites. He "fulfilled" the Law, putting aside its traditional ceremonies and worship, by inculcating a few spiritual principles; as Nature strips the dead leaves from the trees in the spring time by sending through their branches currents of fresh, vigorous sap. To us, reading the Gospel at this distance, it is clear what His intentions were from the beginning. He declared that old things had passed away; that he made all things new; He taught that the old bottles could not contain the new wine; foretold the desolation of the old house, and affirmed that many should come from the East and the West and sit down with the patriarchs in the kingdom of God. The single utterance: "The hour cometh and now is, when the true worshipers shall worship the Father in spirit and in truth, for the Father seeketh such to worship Him,"* involved the expansion of the old ethnic faith, the abrogation of the local worship at Jerusalem, and the disuse of the Hebrew ritual. But He was content to assert the principle and leave it to do its work. Even Pentecost did not unseal the eyes of his disciples to the far-reaching applications and consequences of the saying. Nor did these disciples understand the ultimate bearings of what took place on that day. Peter recited two oracles

---

* John iv: 23.

from the Old Testament: "And it shall come to pass, that whosoever shall call upon the name of the Lord shall be saved;*" "The promise is to you and to your children, and to all that are afar off, even as many as the Lord our God shall call;" but it is plain that neither he nor his auditors understood the full significance of the language. Under the guidance of the Spirit, he preached far better than he knew. To us, the Pentecost is the close of the dispensation of Law and the beginning of the dispensation of Grace, but the Apostles did not firmly grasp this view until some years later. We may wonder that they were so slow to perceive the bearings of things, but we must remember how thorough was the legal discipline of the Jews, how firmly the cake of custom was cemented, and that their point of view was very different from our own.

Third, the Pentecost brought into the Christian communion a new element. Thus far, it had consisted wholly of Palestinian Jews, the "Hebrews" of Acts vi: 1. But now a number of Hellenistic Jews, Jews of the Dispersion, were converted. In common with the class to which they belonged, they spoke the Greek language, read the Scriptures in the Septuagint Version, and shared some of the liberal tendencies of the Greek mind; on all of which accounts, like their class, they were the subjects of much dislike and even enmity to their more orthodox brethren. What is more, probably some Jewish proselytes, Gentiles who had been circumcised, were among the three thousand Pentecostal converts. Certainly many proselytes were then in Jerusalem,† and soon after we find one who was an influential member of the Church, Nicolas of Antioch.‡ The new element was destined to play an important part in the future history of the Church; its introduction is a fact of great moment.

---

* Acts ii: 21, 39.   † *Ibid.* ii: 10.   ‡ *Ibid.* vi: 5.

"The great question which the Church in the Apostolic Age was required to consider and determine," says Prof. Fisher, "was the relation of Christianity to the ritual Law of the Old Testament." He also describes the agitation produced by this question as a "commotion," "a great conflict," and says "the sound of this great conflict reverberates through no inconsiderable portion of the New Testament Scriptures." He further describes it as "the question whether Christianity was, in its real nature, a spiritual, and so a universal, religion, or only an improved sect or phase of Judaism."* In fact the questions of first moment in that age were but two in number: Shall Christianity gain a firm foothold in the world? What shall Historical Christianity be? The original deposit of doctrine was indeed of divine origin, but it remained to be seen what the human mind, and especially the Jewish mind, would do with it. Stated in other words the second question was: Shall the Jewish or the Grecian mind give Christianity its historical shaping and impulse? Wrapped up in this question was the relation, in the Gospel, of the Gentile to the Jew. Fortunately, the nucleus of the Church was homogeneous; fortunately, too, the Church had become somewhat enlarged and consolidated before the question became troublesome, but, at the same time, it demanded an answer as soon as the Christians were prepared to deal with it.

We hear the first angry note of the long controversy where we should least look for it. The condition of the Church in Jerusalem rendered necessary a community of goods. "All that believed were together, and had all things common; and sold their possessions and goods, and parted them to all men as every man had need."† This is one of

---

* *Supernatural Origin of Christianity*, New York, 1867, pp. 205, 6.
† Acts ii: 44, 45.

the most striking and beautiful aspects of the primitive Church: it is a part of the Apostles' fellowship. Sad commentary on human nature that, in the midst of this love and concord, the first note of the bitter strife should be heard! By and by, "when the number of the disciples was multiplied, there arose a murmuring of the Grecians against the Hebrews, because their widows were neglected in the daily ministration."* These "Grecians" were Hellenistic Jews, and the "Hebrews" of whom they complained were Jews of Palestine. Why these widows were neglected, the historian does not tell us; but it is almost certain that the neglect was due to selfishness and caste-feeling. The murmuring led to the appointment of the Seven, commonly regarded as the first deacons, as superintendents of the daily distribution. It is clear that the Seven, next to the Apostles, were the men of widest influence in the growing community. What is more, they all bear Greek names."† We cannot, however, infer that they were all "Grecians," for it was common for "Hebrews" to bear Greek names.‡ But one of them was both a Hellenist and a proselyte, Nicolas of Antioch; and it is reasonable to suppose that several of the others were Hellenists. It would be very strange if of seven Jews having Greek names, selected under such circumstances especially, only one was a "Grecian." The whole transaction warrants us in inferring, either that the contest between the "Hebrews" and the "Grecians" had not become very sharp as yet, or that the latter had a very great influence in the Jerusalem Church; in fact, there is no opposition between the two inferences, and both are no doubt true. The unhappy strife probably grew more out of an old class-prejudice than of a present theological difference; for as yet the

---

* Acts vi: 1. † *Ibid.* vi: 5.
‡ For example, Andrew and Philip in the Apostolic College.

Christians cannot be said to regard religious questions from a standpoint distinctly theological.* Probably the appointment of the Seven mollified the feeling that had arisen, and temporarily composed the mind of the Church. Before we hear the next note of the controversy, the Christian flock has once more been smitten and scattered.

The young deacon Stephen was a fervent preacher of the Gospel. He was a Hellenist, at all events of Hellenistic temper and tendencies. He carried the Christian argument into the camp of those Hellenistic Jews who had not embraced Christianity.† In his controversies with the leaders of the foreign synagogues, he presented the Gospel in a bolder and freer spirit than had yet been done; so much so, that he incurred the charge of blaspheming the Temple and the Law, of teaching that Jesus of Nazareth would destroy the holy place, and change the customs which Moses had delivered‡—a false charge in the light in which the false witnesses exhibited it, but that grew out of what Stephen had said concerning the relations of the old and new faiths. The preaching of the proto-martyr gives us the first glimpse of a catholic Christianity that is consciously grasped by the one who preaches it. The memorable defense which provoked his death, is in the same tone. It breathes throughout the spirit of the Apostle to the Gentiles; it has justly been called the "proem" to the Epistles of Paul. He follows the historical method of discussion. "His denunciations of local worship," says Dean Stanley, "the stress which he lays on

---

* "A murmuring of the Grecians against the Hebrews, or of the Hebrews against the Grecians, had been of common occurrence for at least two centuries; and notwithstanding the power of the Divine Spirit, none will wonder that it broke out again even among those who had become obedient to the doctrine of Christ."—*Life and Epistles of St. Paul*, vol. i. p. 66.

† Acts vi: 9.   ‡ *Ibid.* vi: 13, 14.

the spiritual side of the Jewish history, his freedom in treating that history, the very terms of expression which he uses, are all Pauline." Stephen's declaration, "Howbeit the Most High dwelleth not in temples made with hands" was, perhaps, the germ of the Apostle's grander burst at Athens: "God that made the world and all things therein, seeing that he is Lord of heaven and earth, dwelleth not in temples made with hands; neither is worshiped with men's hands, as though he needed anything." The Deacon was the forerunner of the Apostle, and had he lived he might have performed the work that Paul performed.

The persecution that followed the death of Stephen, widened the breach between Christianity and Judaism. It put an end to the *quasi*-understanding between the Christians and the Pharisees. It led to a great territorial enlargement of the Church, and also to an enlargement of the Christian consciousness. Whether the Gospel had previously extended beyond the Holy City, we cannot tell. However this may be, it now travels to the borders of Judea, and passes them as soon as they are reached. "They that were scattered abroad went everywhere preaching the Word."*

IV.—SAMARIA.

Philip, one of the Seven, went to one of the cities of Samaria and began preaching to the people. His reception is shown by the words of the historian: "And there was great joy in that city. * * When they believed Philip preaching the things concerning the Kingdom of

---

* Acts viii: 4.

God, and the name of Jesus Christ, they were baptized, both men and women." What had occurred was soon reported in Jerusalem. "Now when the Apostles which were at Jerusalem heard that Samaria had received the Word of God, they sent unto them Peter and John," who, on their arrival, sanctioned and consummated the work that Philip had so auspiciously begun. What is more, on their return the two Apostles preached the Gospel in many Samaritan villages. Apostles had now been witnesses unto Christ in Samaria.*

In his last interview with His disciples, our Lord assigned to Samaria a position in the history of evangelization intermediate between "Jerusalem and Judea" on the one hand, and "the uttermost part of the earth" on the other. This position was intermediate in a doctrinal, as well as in a geographical and a chronological, sense. Here the Christian mind temporarily halted as it moved from the Jewish to the Gentile conception of the Gospel.

Why were Peter and John sent from Jerusalem to Samaria? The answer is easy if we keep in mind the relations of the Jews to the Samaritans, and the state of the Christian consciousness previous to this transaction. The Jew hated the Samaritan with an intense, bitter hatred. We read in one of the Evangelists, that "the Jews have no dealings with the Samaritans;"† and in the Talmud: "He that takes the bread of a Samaritan is like him who eats the flesh of swine. No Israelite may receive a Samaritan as a proselyte; the accursed people shall have no part in the resurrection of the dead." No doubt this feeling had been somewhat softened in the cases of the Apostles, but their minds still moved in the old Jewish orbit. Up to this time none but circumcised Jews had been received

---

* Acts viii: 8, 12.   † John iv: 9.

into the new fold; and few, if any, of the disciples saw that Christianity was to be propagated without regard to race lines. Under these circumstances it was inevitable that Philip's proceedings in Samaria should be questioned. If any of the more pronounced "Hebrew" brethren lingered in Jerusalem, they would denounce his action as irregular and unauthorized. Added to the fact that the Samaritans did not belong to the theocratic race, was their proverbial credulousness, excitability, and liability to be led about by such pretenders as Simon the sorcerer. In consequence, the simple announcement, "Samaria has received the Word of God," was enough to fill all disciples with apprehension, and most with alarm and hostility. Philip had taken a step forward, and it was regarded as of questionable propriety, at least so far as to call for examination. Accordingly, the Apostolic College sent two of their number to Samaria, to obtain a fuller knowledge of what had transpired, to repudiate the work if it appeared irregular or defective, to set the seal of their approval upon it if it appeared legitimate and authorized. In the latter event, some ulterior events would follow. The Samaritan converts would be confirmed in the faith, and the Apostles would be the better able to mollify the feeling of hostility on the part of the stricter brethren—thus aiding to keep the unity of the Spirit in the bond of peace. In the former event, the nascent Church would be relieved of scandals growing out of an ill-considered act. Two things would predispose the Apostles to look with favor upon what had been done—the Samaritans were a circumcised people, and, after their own fashion, they kept the Law—both legal points, but for that reason all the more important to the Jewish mind. In the estimation of the Jew, the Samaritan stood on a different footing from the Gentile. The Jew's hostility to the Samaritan was caused by three facts: he was of mongrel blood; he repudiated all of the Old Testament except the Pentateuch; and he had a rival temple and worship on Mount Gerizim, that constantly challenged the exclusiveness of Jerusalem. Hence, the Jew's antipathy was of a sectarian rather than of a race character, and it would be the less felt when it was proposed to merge both Jerusalem and Gerizim in a more comprehensive worship. Nor must we omit from this summary of influences some facts in the ministry of Christ. He had set at defiance the prevailing Jewish antipathy. One of His parables turned on a contrast between a good Samaritan and an unmerciful priest and Levite. He spent some time in or near Sychar, where He uttered some of His most pregnant truths, and He rebuked His disciples when they proposed to destroy a Samaritan village that had slighted their Master. On the other hand He said of the same people: "Ye worship ye know not what. We know what we worship, for salvation is of the Jews;"* and, when sending out the Twelve for the first time, he instructed them: "Into any city of the Samaritans enter ye not."† These facts touched the Samaritan problem at different points, and probably tended somewhat to confuse the Christian mind. Arrived in the city, Peter and John made inquiry into the work that had been done; and the descent of the Holy Spirit, in answer to prayer, sealed the transaction by removing any lingering doubts as to whether it was divinely approved. The Apostles sanctioned what the Deacon had done; and the right of the Samaritans to a home in the Church, so far as we know, was nevermore questioned. Their conversion was the first breach in "the middle wall of partition." It marks a step in the enlargement of the Church, and also

---

* John iv: 22. † Matthew x: 5.

in the unfolding of the Christian conception of the Gospel.*

*No historian or commentator known to me has put the conversion of the Samaritans in the proper light. They all feel obliged to answer the question—Why were Peter and John sent to Samaria? and all more or less widely miss the answer. According to what may be called the High Church or sacerdotal view, Philip—since he was not an apostle—could not confer the gift of the Holy Ghost; and it therefore became necessary to send Apostles—to whom this power was confined—to complete what he had commenced. This is a part of the doctrine of confirmation. But Ananias—who was not an apostle—imparted the Spirit to Saul, (Acts ix: 17.) Neander says: "At all events, it is evident that the manner in which the Gospel gained entrance among the Samaritans must have appeared to the two Apostles as defective," ("Planting and Training," N. Y., 1865, p. 61); and Schaff: "The Apostles, therefore, sent two of their number—Peter and John—to Samaria, to examine the matter and supply what was wanting," ("Apostolic Church," N. Y., 1868, p. 215.)

In reply to this view it may be urged: (1) That everything necessary to these conversions could have been supplied by Philip; (2) There is no reason to suppose that the Apostles which remained at Jerusalem knew there was a "defect," even if there were one, since they had simply heard that "Samaria had received the Word of God." The only "defect" that was likely to strike the mind of disciples at Jerusalem, was in Philip's preaching to the Samaritans and baptizing them. There is no reason to suppose that the visit had reference to an extraordinary impartation of the Spirit. Lechler's remark has some force: "The two Apostles ascertained, after their arrival, that, by imparting the Holy Ghost, they could materially strengthen the new converts, and aid in the work of maintaining the moral purity and uprightness of the congregation, in view of the equivocal purposes of the Sorcerer," (in Lange's "Acts of Apostles.") Alford says: "Our Lord's command (Acts i: 8) had removed all doubt as to Samaria being a legitimate field for preaching, and Samaritan converts being admissible," ("New Testament for English Readers.") As well argue that the same command had put an end to all scruples in regard to the admission of the Gentiles. It has been shown that the earliest disciples *did* expect the nations to be converted to Christ, but that they first expected them to put themselves in proper relation to the Law. The Jewish prejudice yielded first in the case of the Samaritans, for reasons stated above. Alford also thinks it was necessary for "the Apostles to perform [in Samaria] their especial part as the divinely appointed Founders of the Church." According to this view, their services would have been in requisition everywhere, and nothing final could have been done without them.

SAMARIA. 57

As a sort of pendant to the foregoing history, appears the account of the Ethiopian eunuch. Here again Philip is the instrument in the hand of Providence. Acting under the divine direction, he took the desert road that led south from Jerusalem to Gaza. When he had proceeded some distance on his way, he fell in with an Ethiopian who had been to Jerusalem to worship, and who, now returning home in his chariot, was reading the prophet Isaiah. Being invited to join the distinguished stranger, Philip preached Christ to him, and concluded by baptizing him. Only one feature of this case invites our attention here. According to the ancient tradition of the Church, this Ethiopian was "the first fruits of the Gentiles throughout the world."* Much current assertion to the contrary, I hold this tradition to be strictly true. Some writers assert that the Ethiopian was a Jew, resting the proposition on the facts that he had been to Jerusalem to worship, and was reading the Scriptures as he journeyed homeward. But this is no evidence; for it is well known that both these acts were sometimes engaged in by pious Gentiles who were favorably disposed to the Jewish religion.† What is more, the fact that he was an eunuch negatives the inference that he was a Jew. The Law rigidly excluded all such persons from the congregation of the Lord.‡ But, it is replied, the term "eunuch" sometimes means a "court-officer" merely, and not a man who has undergone bodily mutilation. This must be granted as a fact of history; but then it must be shown that this is the meaning of the term in the present case. If it could be proved that the Ethiopian was a Jew, this objection could be waived; but it cannot be waived to make room

---

* Eusebius, *Ecclesiastical History*, ii: 1.
† See John xii: 2.
‡ Deuteronomy xxiii: 1.

for an unsupported hypothesis. In addition to the force of the first meaning of the word itself, it must be added that the Ethiopian was the minister of a female sovereign, which greatly increases the probability that the word is here used in its literal sense.

It is undeniable that the first and the natural interpretation of the history is—the Eunuch was a Gentile. The theory that he was not, is resorted to to prop up another theory that is just as unfounded, viz: Cornelius and his household were the first fruits of the Gentiles. Perhaps it is worth while to add, both these theories are a part of a certain general view of the evangelical history that, in some sense, puts the conversion of Cornelius on a par with Pentecost. The Eunuch could not have been a Jew by birth, nor a proselyte of righteousness; the utmost that the facts warrant, is the inference that he was a proselyte of the gate, and this no doubt he was. He and Cornelius belonged to the same class, but it was his good fortune first to be introduced into the kingdom of God. Accordingly, his conversion was a new step in the advance.*

If this view of the transaction on the road to Gaza be correct, the question arises, Did it provoke any comment or arouse any hostility on the part of the stricter disciples?

---

* Lechler, Alford, and many others support the above view. The following is Alford's note:

"The very general use of eunuchs in the East for filling offices of confidence, and the fact that this man was minister to a female sovereign, makes it probable that he was literally a eunuch. If not so, the word would hardly have been expressed. No difficulty arises from Deut. xxiii: 1, for no inference can be drawn from the history further than that he may have been a proselyte of the gate, in whose case the prohibition would not apply. Nay; the whole occurrence seems to have had one design, connected with this fact. The walls of partition were one after another being thrown down: the Samaritans were already in full possession of the Gospel: it was next to be shown that none of those physical incapacities which excluded from the congregation of the Lord under the old covenant, form any bar to Christian baptism and the inheritance among believers; and thus the way gradually to be paved for the great and as yet incomprehensible truth of Galatians iii: 28."

SAMARIA. 59

Here we are left wholly to conjecture. It may not have been immediately reported. The "Hebrews" may have reconciled themselves to it on the ground that it was an isolated case, and that the Ethiopian had returned to his home; or their scruples may have been quieted by the preacher's telling them that he acted under the divine guidance. All things considered, it is not likely that the conversion of the Eunuch aroused any strong opposition. If it had, Luke would probably have recorded the fact. At all events, there is no evidence that it aided in any respect to settle the question of the rights of the Gentiles under the new dispensation.*

We pass now to two series of events, each independent of the other, but both standing in the same relation to the dispersion of the disciples from Jerusalem, in which the question, "What is the relation of Law and Gospel?" assumed the most threatening proportions. These are narrated in the X and XI chapters of the Acts of the Apostles, and are more important than any other transactions in the whole book, except those of Pentecost. These chapters contain the two head springs of Historic or Gentile Christianity. It is highly probable, if not certain, that the conversion of the Eunuch antedates these events; but the Eunuch immediately returned to his home at Meroe, high up the Nile, and we can trace no stream of Christian influence to him. One of the two springs is Cæsarea, the other Antioch.

---

* Renan says this case became a "precedent of great weight," having "eminent dogmatic value." He says, "It was an argument for those who thought that the doors of the new church ought to be opened to all." ("The Apostles," N. Y., 1866, p. 159.) This is possible, though there is no evidence that such is the case. On the other hand, there are some negative considerations, as above, to show that it attracted little attention at the time, though the tradition preserved by Eusebius shows that it was emphasized by the later Church.

V.—THE CONVERSION OF CORNELIUS.

All that had transpired had not taught the Apostle Peter the real nature of the divine kingdom. He sufficiently understood the work of Christ and His relations to His people, but he failed to understand the relations of the two dispensations. What he had seen in Samaria had considerably enlarged his mental horizon, but he was not yet ready to open the doors of the Church to the Gentiles. He was an honest man, teachable although prejudiced, ready to be taught and guided by inspiration and the logic of events; but proposing to limit the Christian fellowship to Jews, Samaritans, and such Gentiles as should embrace the Law. He may be said to represent the average Christian opinion of the time. There was a more liberal and progressive section of the Church, made up of proselytes and Jews of the Dispersion, who were prepared to admit the Gentiles to all the rights and privileges of the Church without question. And there was also a third class, made up of Jewish bigots, the Judaizers of a later day, who never had comprehended, and never would comprehend, the fact that Christianity was a new religion. At this stage of the history of the Church, all the disciples, without regard to their various shades of thought, conformed strictly to the Jewish customs, so far as they had opportunity; retaining the fixed hours of prayer, attending the Temple worship, and observing the sacred festivals.

Two divine revelations, one to himself and one to Cornelius, a Roman centurion stationed at Cæsarea, at last taught Peter that "God is no respecter of persons, but in every nation he that feareth Him and worketh righteousness, is accepted with Him."* Thus taught that every person

---

*Acts x: 34, 5.

who seeks the Lord is an accepted seeker, without regard to race, condition, or his relation to Judaism, the Apostle recited the main facts of the Gospel to the Centurion, his "kinsmen and near friends;" and when the Holy Ghost fell on them who heard the Word, as on the Jewish Christians "at the beginning," he "commanded them to be baptized in the name of the Lord."* Jerusalem was in constant communication with Cæsarea, and almost immediately "the Apostles and brethren that were in Judea heard that the Gentiles had also received the Word of God."† Peter's act threw the Church into the greatest consternation, but gave a new impulse to Christianity. On his return to Jerusalem, "they that were of the circumcision contended with him," charging: "Thou wentest in to men uncircumcised, and didst eat with them."‡ The Apostle had committed the offence described by himself when first he met Cornelius: "Ye know how that it is an unlawful thing for a man that is a Jew to keep company or come unto one of another nation."§ No man can understand the conflict in the early Church, who does not perceive the meaning of this charge, and the spirit in which it was made.

In the first place, the description "they that were of the circumcision," can not refer to circumcision in a physical sense; for as yet, all the disciples in Judea bore that mark in the flesh. It is not to be understood objectively, but subjectively; it is a description of those disciples who were of a particular cast of thought. The men who complained of Peter were great sticklers for circumcision, and the Mosaic Law in general. It must be remarked again, that the terms "Hebrew" and "Grecian," from denoting descent and external condition, had taken on a certain mental and religious coloring. In the second place, neither in word nor in principle did the Law contain such

---

* Acts x: 44, 8.   † *Ibid.* xi: 1.   ‡ *Ibid.* xi: 2–3.   § *Ibid.* x: 2.

an injunction as the Apostle was charged with violating. The prohibition to eat with a Gentile was a part of Jewish tradition, one of the commandments of men that the Rabbis inculcated with so much strictness and authority. It was all the more absurd and contrary to the genius of Old Testament religion in the case of Cornelius, "a devout man, and one that feared God with all his house." The fact that Peter shared this prejudice until taught to call "nothing unclean that God had cleansed," shows that the early Church was not only under the influence of Judaism but also of Rabbinism. Nor, in the third place, did these Judeo-Christians mean to censure the Apostle for preaching to Gentiles and baptizing them. That the heathen were to partake of the benefits of the Gospel, had been understood all along. But Peter had not insisted on the circumcision of the Centurion and his induction into the Jewish Church as a condition of evangelization; he had established fraternal fellowship with those outside of the covenant of circumcision; and in this consisted the Judaizing principle that so long disturbed the peace of the Church. Had Peter made Jews as well as disciples of Jesus, of the converts at Cæsarea, no charge would have been prefered against him. So far from the Judaizing Christians understanding that the Law was a "schoolmaster to bring men to Christ," they rather thought the Gospel a schoolmaster to bring the heathen to Moses. But Peter "rehearsed the matter from the beginning" with such effect, as not only to silence, for the time being, his censors, but to cause the congregation to glorify God, by exclaiming: "Then hath God also to the Gentiles granted repentance unto life!" To their minds, this was a revelation as new and unexpected as the one made to Peter himself on the housetop at Joppa.

But why should the conversion of Gentiles in Cæsarea create such a commotion, when, so far as we can judge, the conversion of the Eunuch attracted little or no attention? The conversion of the Ethiopian, from one point of view, would seem much more likely to shock Jewish prejudices; for he was not only a Gentile, but had suffered emasculation. The hypothesis that his case was not reported, casually suggested above, can hardly be entertained; for Philip, the Evangelist by pre-eminence, would not be slow to spread the news of the conquests of grace. A full answer to the question lies in the following facts: The Eunuch was one, the Centurion and his company were many; the Eunuch was baptized in an out-of-the-way place and immediately went on his way homeward, while the Centurion lived in a populous city. The transaction in Cæsarea was bruited around in such a way as greatly to scandalize the legal purists at Jerusalem. It gave the non-believing Jew an opportunity to say to his believing friend or kinsman: "You now see into what company your new guides are leading you;" and we must not suppose that at this time the Jewish Christian was indifferent to orthodox Jewish opinion. What is more, probably the Evangelist had not entered into as intimate social relationships with the Ethiopian as the Apostle had with the Italian. Finally, those "which were of the circumcision" could dispose of the one case by calling it sporadic, exceptional, and unauthorized, a plea that would not lie in the other. They could more easily disavow an act performed by an evangelist than an act performed by the most influential Apostle in the whole college. In the words of Dean Alford: "The stress of the narrative in Chapter X consists in the miscellaneous admission of all the Gentile company of Cornelius, and their official reception into the Church, by that Apostle to whom was especially given the power."* It remains to

---

*New Testament for English Readers.

examine the bearings of the foregoing history on the great question that so profoundly disturbed the Church in the Apostolic Age.

It reveals the existence within the Church of two kinds of opinion and character. The line of separation was not yet so closely drawn as it soon became; but we recognize here in germ the Judaizers and the catholic Christians of a later time. We have no data from which to determine their relative unmbers, though the latter are in the ascendency even in Jerusalem. Were it not for subsequent events, we might think that the triumph of the catholic party, the triumph of grace, rather, was complete and final; that the question was settled forever, at least for Jerusalem; but these events, soon to be traced, show that the controversy, so far from being ended, had only commenced. The more pronounced Judaic party yielded only temporarily; long fixed prejudices soon revived; the old fires burned fiercer than ever. What had been gained? Considerably less than some thoughtful men, generally well informed in the Scriptures, seem to think. According to a very common view, the Judeo-Gentile question sprang into being fully developed on the conversion of Cornelius, but was soon and effectually settled. This view further grants that a few Jewish zealots continued to disturb the peace of the Church with their outcry for the "fleshly" ordinances, but that the conversion of Cornelius effectually demolished the "middle wall of partition." To reason thus is to exaggerate what had been done. Cornelius, his "kinsmen and near friends," are in the Christian fellowship; Peter's eyes have been opened; he now sees the comprehension of the commission that his Master had laid upon his heart; a most important lesson had been taught those disciples who are teachable; the leading members of the Church are committed to a principle; a precedent has been set that will not be forgotten; henceforth to deny a Gentile admission to the Church on confession of faith and baptism will be a step backward. Still the Gentile's position in the Church is not fully determined. Shall he be the equal in all respects of his Jewish brother? The "middle wall of partition," once breached in Samaria, again on the road to Gaza, is now "broken down" much more thoroughly in Cæsarea; but it still stands in formidable proportions, and will continue to stand until the actors in Cæsarea and Jerusalem have passed away. But questions of secondary nature will be settled in course of time. The Church will never disavow the action of Peter. The Apostle to whom the keys had been committed, has opened the doors of the Church to the Gentiles, and no man can shut them.

VI.—THE CONVERSION OF GREEKS IN ANTIOCH.

The second series of events mention at the close of Section IV. introduces us to a new theatre of activity, and one very different from any hitherto considered, Antioch, the opulent capital of Syria. Before tracing these events, we must glance at the city itself. I shall borrow some colors from the palette of Renan.*

Situated on the Orontes where that river breaks through the mountain-wall formed by the junction of the Taurus and the Lebanon, the site of Antioch was one of the most picturesque in the world. Geographically, it was the gate of the East; and from the founding of the Greek Empire in Asia to the building of Constantinople, the city of Antiochus was the Eastern metropolis. It abounded in public works and works of art, constructed and gathered by the

---

* The Apostles, Chap. XII.

Seleucid princes. Both nature and art contributed to its adornment. Its population, more than half a million in number, was the wash of the Eastern world. Although a Greek city it was compounded of the most diverse elements. In the words of Renan:

"It was an inconceivable medley of merry-andrews, quacks, buffoons, magicians, miracle-mongers, sorcerers, priests, impostors; a city of races, games, dances, processions, fetes, debauches, of unbridled luxury, of all the follies of the East, of the most unhealthy superstitions, and of the fanaticisms of the orgy." "The great corso which traversed the city was like a theatre, where rolled, day after day, the waves of a trifling, light-headed, changeable, insurrection-loving populace—a populace sometimes *spirituel*, occupied with romps, parodies, squibs, impertinences of all sorts."

But there were solider and more stable elements than these: had there not been so great a community could not have existed. "The city was very literary, but literary only in the literature of rhetoricians." It was "one of the places in the world where race was most intermingled with race." Very naturally religion was as parti-colored as the populace. "Syrian levity, Babylonian charlatanism, and all the impostures of Asia, mingled at this limit of the two worlds, had made Antioch a capital of lies and the sink of every description of infamy." But polytheism and idol-worship did not bear universal sway. Antioch was the seat of a long-established, numerous, and powerful colony of Jews. It was also the theatre of a well-organized and efficient Jewish propagandism. Proselytes were numerous, and many of the heathen who had not been converted to Judaism were more or less influenced by Jewish thought and religion. Nicolas, one of the Seven, it will be remembered, was a proselyte of Antioch. Nor must it be forgotten that the proselyte readily received a liberal type of Christianity. He was never found on the side of the Judaizers.

Here were a soil and an atmosphere very different from

the soil and atmosphere of Jerusalem. If Christianity were once planted in this great capital, it could not be kept within the limits to which it was confined by the Jewish mind; its growth would be more free and luxuriant. What is more, the Gospel would soon reach such a city. It would seek out the Jewish colony; or, if not, a city that gave a welcome home to every form of faith and every type of worship would invite it from sheer levity and wantonness. Probably there was no center of population in the East that the conservative Jewish disciples would so reluctantly see Christianity enter. Accordingly, Antioch now became the home of what Renan calls a "young, innovating, and ardent Church, full of the future, because it was composed of the most diverse elements." It was here that Christianity found its name; here that its great missionary enterprises began; here that it learned the language in which its Holy Oracles were written; here that disciples in large numbers first awoke to a full realization of what Christianity involved. To quote Renan once more: "It was on the shores of the Orontes that the religious fusion of races dreamed of by Jesus, or to speak more correctly, by six centuries of prophets, became a reality." Important as was the conversion of Cornelius, in the strictly historical sense the planting of the new faith in the Gate of the East far transcended it. The persecution that sent the Gospel to the Samaritans, to the Eunuch, and to Cæsarea, sent it also to the Syrian capital. The primitive record runs as follows:

"Now they which were scattered abroad upon the persecution that arose about Stephen, traveled as far as Phenice, and Cyprus, and Antioch, preaching the word to none but unto the Jews only. And some of them were men of Cyprus and Cyrene, which, when they were come to Antioch, spake unto the Grecians, preaching the Lord Jesus. And the hand of the Lord was with them: and a great number believed and turned unto the Lord."*

* Acts xi: 19-21.

This modest narrative of a great transaction calls for two remarks:

1. It is impossible to make out a definite chronology of the Book of Acts, especially the first half of the book. Events do not always follow each other in the order of time, and it is sometimes impossible to determine their precise chronological relations. The persecution following the death of Stephen was followed by the conversion of the Samaritans, and this again by the conversion of the Eunuch and the Centurion; the two latter, no doubt, in the order in which the historian gives them. But the record given above, the preaching in Antioch, stands in the same relation to Acts viii: 4, the dispersion of the disciples from Jerusalem, that the preaching in Samaria does; though we cannot be certain as to the length of time involved in either case. Acts viii: 5-40, ix: 32-43, and x; and Acts xi: 19-21, are two parallel series of events, co-ordinate in rank and largely contemporaneous. The Gospel may have been preached in Antioch as soon as it was to the Eunuch, or even to the Samaritans; and it is almost certain that it was preached in that city before Peter opened the doors of the Church to Gentiles in Cæsarea. But waiving this point, it is beyond question that what has now been done in Antioch is altogether independent of Peter's action in the case of Cornelius. However these events may have occurred in the order of time, they are wholly distinct and separate in aspects, consequences, and in immediate causes; though both alike are the results of the later and more enlarged conception of the Gospel.

2. The persons called "Grecians" in this passage (following the common version) do not belong to the same class as the "Grecians" of chapter vi. Those were Hellenistic Jews, these are Gentiles. The respective Greek words are 'Ἑλληνιστής and Ἕλλην; and both words are found in this passage in different manuscripts. On the whole,

there is about as much manuscript authority for the one reading as the other; but the sense of the passage shows that the latter is the proper word. Evidently the class named in verse 20 is logically opposed to the class named in verse 19; while "Grecian" gives no such opposition, since, as shown in Part First, it is a species under Jew. Greek, or Gentile, is opposed to Jew; "Grecian," to "Hebrew." What is more, the Gospel had been preached to the "Grecians" ever since the day of Pentecost, and if they were the class here referred to the passage would mark no new step in the advance, and would have no meaning. No doubt the preaching to "Jews only" in Antioch involved both "Hebrews" and "Grecians." Again, the conversion of Greeks in the metropolis of Syria was going a step further than the conversion of the Eunuch and the Centurion. Both the latter were religious men, recognizing the God of the Old Covenant, "proselytes of the gate," while the Antiochian converts were undoubtedly heathen idolators who came into the fellowship, not from prayer and study of the Scriptures, but from the disgusting rites of Oriental worship.* While the conversion of Cornelius and his household stands as the formal, representative, and divinely authorized introduction of the Gentiles to the Church, the conversion of these Greeks in Antioch, in some points of view, is the more important transaction. Antioch was the home of the younger Church, the head spring of catholic Christianity.

Once more we are ready to move forward. When tidings of what had taken place in Syria "came unto the ears of the Church which was in Jerusalem" "they sent forth Barnabas, that he should go as far as Antioch."† Why Barnabas was sent, we are not told. It is safe to infer that the tidings received in Jerusalem caused grave apprehen-

---

* See Lightfoot on *Gal.*, p. 291.   † Acts xi: 22.

sion in the Church, and that this Son of Consolation was sent to ascertain the facts and to act in the light of developments. For the most part, his mission was similar to that of Peter and John to Samaria. But with whatever intent he was sent, the mission of Barnabas was providential. He was a Hellenist of the neighboring island of Cyprus,* and belonged to the more progressive and evangelical section of the Mother Church. Besides, he was a "good man," "full of the Holy Ghost" and of faith, prepared to interpret all providential developments. Recognizing the work as one that proceeded from the "grace of God," he threw into it the full power and fervor of his nature. He saw that "a great and effectual door" had been opened, and he immediately pressed into it.

While the transactions already enumerated had been transpiring in various quarters—that is, sometime between the scattering of the disciples and the admission of the Gentiles—an event had happened one noonday near the city of Damascus; an event so important that the author of the Acts interrupts his narrative of general evangelical operations to narrate it: it was the conversion of Saul of Tarsus, marked from the death of Stephen as the spiritual successor of the young Deacon, a "chosen vessel to bear the name of Christ before the Gentiles, and kings, and the children of Israel." Barnabas had the penetrative sympathy which enabled him to see that the conversion of the young Pharisee was genuine, and the courage to vouch for him at a time when many hesitated and even the Apostles were in doubt† Several years of meditation in the solitude of the East, and of evangelical labor, have fully prepared Saul for his great work among the Gentiles. His opportunity has also come. Barnabas now seeks him in the city of Tarsus, finds him and brings him to Antioch. Here the blessed

---

* Acts iv: 36. † *Ibid.* ix: 27.

work goes on. "And it came to pass that a whole year they assembled themselves with the church, and taught much people."* Here the disciples found the name by which they were to be henceforth known. "And the disciples were called Christians first in Antioch." The name was bestowed by man and not by God, and its bestowal was an historical affirmation of the fact that the Gospel is a new religion and not a phase of Judaism. Prof. Fisher has fitly said, "Then the disciples first began to be called Christians; and properly, for then they first became Christians in the full sense,—a body distinct from the Jews."

What has now taken place in Cæsarea and in Antioch shows that Christ's religion has at length found its way out of Judea into the great world. As one follows its fortunes on this larger stage of action, he cannot help wondering what its fate would have been, and what name it would have borne, if it had been forever confined within the rigid boundaries of Judaism.

VII.—THE COUNCIL OF JERUSALEM.

The Church in Antioch was so rich in gifts that it was much more than equal to the edification of itself. Acting under the guidance of the Spirit it "separated" Barnabas and Saul for a missionary work among the heathen,† the history of which need not be here followed. The next occurrence in the direct line of our present inquiry, is the arrival of some persons in Antioch who are called "certain men which came down from Judea."‡ The words "from Judea," as Lechler remarks, "do not simply contain a geographical notice, but also allude to sentiments and

---

*Acts xi: 25–6.   † *Ibid.* xiii: 1-3.   ‡ *Ibid.* xv: 1.

modes of thought which were pre-eminently Jewish." The burden of their teaching was, "Except ye be circumcised after the manner of Moses, ye cannot be saved." The spirit and tendency of this teaching was clear to the Syrian Christians. If the Jew wished to continue the Levitical rites, he was free to do so; if the Gentile wished to assume them, there was no objection; but to insist on subjecting the Gentiles to these rites as a condition of fellowship, was to deny the sufficiency of grace and to subvert the Gospel. Paul and Barnabas stood forth in unyielding opposition to the demands of the Judaizers. No other men in the Church, either in Judea or Syria, were so well prepared to perceive the bearings of such a doctrine. They were men of broad, catholic sympathy; they saw that such teachings would destroy the peace of the young and growing church in Antioch; not only so, they saw that if the Levitical conception of the Gospel prevailed Christianity was forever confined within the narrow pale of the Jewish nation. They had just returned from a missionary tour in Asia Minor, where they had had the best opportunities to study the whole question; they understood fully the Gentile spirit; and they could not fail to see that, while the Gentiles were hungry for the bread of life, they would never, in considerable numbers, submit to the bondage of the Jewish yoke. Hence, in the minitory tones of the legalists from Judea: "Except ye be circumcised after the manner of Moses, ye cannot be saved," they heard the knell of their fond hopes of evangelization among the heathen, provided they were to be the prevailing sentiment of the Church. The Christian community in Antioch was stirred to its depths. After there had been "no small amount of dissension and disputation, it was decided to refer the matter to the Apostles and Elders at Jerusalem. Chosen messengers accordingly started for that city. The fact that this deputation was "brought on its way by the church," shows the anxiety that filled the minds of the brethren that remained behind; as the further fact that the story of the conversion of the Gentiles caused "great joy" in Phœnicia and Samaria, proves that, however it may have been in Judea, outside of that province the great stream of Christian feeling flowed in the broader and freer channel.

Once arrived in Jerusalem, the messengers had an official reception by the church, at which they freely "declared all things that God had done with them."* Either at this first meeting or at a second one, the question at issue was considered in the general assembly of the church. Some points of great difficulty were involved. Here was an influential embassy from the young, ardent, and powerful congregation in Antioch, pleading for the liberty of conscience and the sufficiency of divine grace. On the other hand stood the pronounced Judaizers, firm, determined, and receiving a certain amount of moral support from the general body of the "Hebrew" Christians. The recital of what had been done in Antioch and in Asia Minor, so far from carrying conviction or silencing opposition, as in the case of Peter's defense on his return from Cæsarea some time before, only aroused a stronger hostility. "There arose up certain of the sect of the Pharisees which believed, saying, that it was needful to circumcise them, and to command them to keep the Law of Moses."† This demand was stronger than the one made in Antioch; there it was only circumcision, here it is the whole Levitical Law. Evidently the Judaizers are confident in the strength of their position. They are surrounded by all the conservative associations of the Holy City, and they receive a certain sympathy from brethren less pronounced in opinion than themselves. They have not ceased to be Pharisees

---

* Acts xv: 4. † *Ibid.* xv: 5.

on coming into the Church. To them Christianity is simply a better form of Judaism. Jerusalem is still the Holy City. The evangelists of the Cross are little more than proselyters. They regard the admission of Gentiles without circumcision as a dangerous and unauthorized innovation. They naturally ask, "Are the courts of the Temple to be forsaken? Can a Jew have a brother who is excused from meeting him at the altar of his fathers? Is Moses to be forgotten and dishonored? Is the time-honored Law to be disregarded? Did not Jesus keep the Law, and did He not enjoin the keeping of it on others? Was not His mission to 'the lost sheep of the House of Israel?'" These Christian Pharisees failed to discriminate between the letter and the spirit. Nor, considering their training, was this so very strange. In the words of Dr. Schaff:

"The idea of such an abstract separation of the moral and ceremonial laws, as is current with many modern theologians, was utterly foreign to them. Their doubts respecting the legality of admitting the uncircumcised into the Christian fellowship, flowed, therefore, very naturally, from their religious training, and were essentially grounded in their conscientiousness and reverence for the Old Testament."*

There is no reason to doubt that, in the beginning, these men were thoroughly sincere; but now that they have taken their positions and the battle has been joined, they begin to exhibit some of the willfulness and fanaticism natural to men of strong prejudices under similar circumstances. Nor are they few in number or weak in influence. The whole history, and especially the decision reached by the council, shows that they are numerous and powerful. Such were the two parties between whom the Apostles and the Elders were to mediate. There was no more anxious moment in the history of the early Church. The responsibility must have been painfully felt. If decision were

---

* *The Apostolic Church*, p. 218.

THE COUNCIL OF JERUSALEM.

given for the Gentiles, the way of the evangelist among the Jews might be hedged up; if for the Judaizers, Gentile evangelization was probably at an end. To the north, the Apostles saw Antioch, Paphos, Iconium, Lystra, the cities of the Greeks to and beyond the Hellespont; around them, they saw their own nation, bound to them by ties of blood, language, and hallowed associations. Although they were guided in their decision by the Holy Spirit, they were not guided in such a way as to relieve their minds of hesitation and anxiety.

But we need not linger longer at the doors of the council chamber. After there had been "much disputing," man with man, Peter rose up and declared that the question involved had been settled by the Holy Spirit in Cæsarea. He demanded: "Why tempt ye God, to put a yoke upon the neck of the disciples which neither our fathers nor we were able to bear?"* Then the two Apostles from Antioch related "what miracles and wonders God had wrought among the Gentiles by them." Profoundly realizing the gravity of the pending question so far as it related to the heathen, they spoke eloquently of the triumphs of Grace, and insisted that the Divine Spirit had sealed their work. The last speaker was James, the brother of the Lord. While the picture of this Apostle given by Hegesippus is no doubt a caricature in part, it cannot be wholly so.† His piety partook of the legal spirit.

---

* Acts xv: 10.

† "This Apostle was consecrated from his mother's womb. He drank neither wine nor fermented liquors, and abstained from animal food. A razor never came upon his head, he never anointed with oil, and never used a bath. He alone was allowed to enter the sanctuary. He never wore woolen, but linen garments. He was in the habit of entering the Temple alone, and was often found upon his bended knees, and interceding for the forgiveness of the people; so that his knees became as hard as camels', in consequence of his habitual supplication and kneeling before God."—Quoted by Eusebius, *Eccl. Hist.* B. II. chap. xxiii.

He was characterized by an excessive austerity, and was unremitting in his ceremonial devotions. After the dispersion of the Apostolic College consequent on the murder of James the brother of John, he appears to have been the most influential person in the Mother Church. James's speech was moderate and conciliatory. Taking his departure from the narrative of Peter, he spoke of the conversion of the Gentiles as an accomplished and approved fact, and closed with proposing a compromise:

"Wherefore my sentence is, that we trouble not them which from among the Gentiles are turned to God. But that we write unto them, that they abstain from pollutions of idols, and from fornication, and from things strangled, and from blood. For Moses of old time hath in every city them that preach him, being read in the Synagogues every Sabbath day." *

He meant, no doubt, by the last statement that the Jewish Christians would continue to obey the Law, and that there was no reason to fear that the claims of the Law-giver would not receive due attention. This basis of settlement, proposed by the staunchest "pillar" of the Church of the Circumcision, was generally acquiesced in; it was put in the form of a decree, and sent by chosen messengers to the churches of Antioch, Syria, and Cilicia; the northern deputation returned home; and events flowed on once more in their wonted channel. But before taking another step forward, we must look more closely into what had been done by the council.

1. The question at issue related only to the Gentile converts. So far as appears, no question had been raised as to the relations of Jewish Christians to the Law. No one had ventured to suggest that a Jew, on conversion to Christ, was free from the yoke of the Old Covenant. All the Jewish disciples obeyed Moses as rigorously as ever.

---

* Acts xv: 19-21.

The greatest stretch of liberty yet conceived by the Christian mind, was involved in the question, whether the Gentile Christian should be required to assume burdens that the Jewish Christian was expected to bear as a matter of course.

2. The church in Jerusalem solemnly disavowed the action of the Judaizers who had visited Antioch. After the salutation in the letter missive, the Apostles, Elders, and brethren went on to say:

"For as much as we have heard that certain that went out from us have troubled you with words, subverting your souls, saying, Ye must be circumcised and keep the Law, to whom we gave no such commandment, it seemed good unto us," etc.*

3. The decision reached was a compromise. It freed the Gentiles from circumcision and the yoke of the ceremonial Law, but it enjoined abstinence from "meats offered to idols, and from blood, and from things strangled, and from fornication." The last was a moral prohibition, but the others were purely legal, well calculated to placate the Palestinian brethren.

4. This decree could not have been considered a finality by the more enlightened members of the council. What was conceded to the Gentiles was without limitation, and with no thought of its revocation; but the purely legal injunctions, it is not supposable, were intended to become a law to the Church. Imposed as concessions to the Jewish conscience, they were probably observed for the time being by those to whom they were immediately addressed. We hear nothing of them later, in Greece or in Italy. On the whole, then, the Gentile Christians have won a substantial advantage on hallowed ground. Discussion has cleared up in some minds a troublesome question; the tacit decision in the case of Cornelius has been reaffirmed in a peculiarly

---

* Acts xv: 24.

weighty and authoritative manner; the schismatical tendency of the more pronounced Judaizers has become more manifest; and a decree has been put forth which will serve more and more to turn the swelling stream of Christian power into the catholic channel. Paul was, no doubt, content with the decision as the best attainable under the circumstances. He now had a firm basis for missionary work among the heathen, and was willing to leave unsettled questions to the logic of events. He knew that the world was larger than Judea, and, perhaps, saw already that the Palestinian Church was merely the John the Baptist of the Gentile Church.

5. On some points the decree was altogether silent. It did not say whether the circumcised and the uncircumcised were to be equal in the new fellowship; or whether the latter were to hold an inferior position, like that of the proselyte in the Jewish Church. It did not say whether the two classes were to flow freely and fraternally together; or whether the Jew was still at liberty to decline social relations with the Gentile. Either intentionally or unintentionally, these points were left undetermined. No doubt the logic of the decree, followed out by an enlightened mind, would do away with all restrictions; but it was quite possible, indeed almost certain, that in that age different minds would arrive at different answers to these questions. De Pressensè goes so far as to say:

"The barrier was lowered, not removed. Thus, no sooner was the decision communicated than it received various interpretations. Paul drew from it inferences which were undoubtedly by implication contained in it, but which were not equally evident to the eyes of all."*

And this no doubt is the simple truth.

6. We must not, therefore, fall into the error of supposing that the question of the age was settled. For the

---

* *Apostolic Era*, p. 139.

time being, the Jewish party was probably overawed; perhaps their numbers somewhat fell off; but they continued powerful for years afterwards. Their flank had been turned, but they had not been driven from the field. Recovering only too soon from their discomfiture, they renewed the conflict and prosecuted it with more bitterness than ever. To the close of his life the Apostle to the Gentiles was doomed to hear the Jewish "dogs" hoarsely baying on his track: "Except ye be circumcised after the manner of Moses, and keep the Law, ye cannot be saved."

7. The history of this controversy shows that, in the primitive church, the Apostolic College was far from being an autocratic power. The word of an Apostle was not always considered the last in a controversy. So true is it, that the figure even of an Apostle becomes larger as you recede from it!

8. It appears from Paul's account of the Council of Jerusalem, that he and Barnabas and the leading Apostles of the circumcision, came to an understanding as to their several fields of labor.* Recognizing that Providence had evidently committed "the Gospel of the uncircumcision" to Paul and "the Gospel of the circumcision" to Peter, the five solemnly covenanted that the two should go unto the heathen, and the three unto the circumcision. It is worth remarking, that we have no other account of the four Apostles, James, Peter, John, and Paul, meeting in consultation over the interests of the Church.

So far was the council of Jerusalem from putting an end to the unhappy strife, that, if possible, it was carried on with more bitterness than ever. Before following the Palestinian Church to its catastrophe, it is necessary to note the widening and intensification of the controversy.

---

* Gal. ii: 1-10.

VIII.—THE MINISTRY OF PAUL.

The life of no other apostle presents so striking a contrast in its earlier and later parts as that of the Apostle to the Gentiles. He was a Hebrew of the Hebrews, and a Pharisee by descent as well as by education. And yet, while the other Apostles, who had been less pronounced Judaists, slowly made their way over the barriers of the old faith, he appears to have cleared them at a single bound. He was the first fully to see the bearings of the pending question. This fact is no doubt explained in part by the boldness of his character and the comprehensiveness of his mind; but it is probable that He who called Saul of Tarsus to be the Apostle to the Gentiles, prepared him for his special work. He was not only markedly successful in evangelizing the heathen, but was also the great bulwark of Gentile rights and liberties in the Gospel. It is not too much to say, that he did more than all the Apostles of the Circumcision put together to resist the Judaizing tendency. In consequence, he became the object of an especial hostility on the part of the Judeo-Christians; and if his name has come down to us loved and honored, it is not because some of them did not do their utmost to blacken it forever. For a full century the controversy went actively on, and so long as Paul lived it always raged most violently along his mighty path.

Antioch was the scene of a second memorable event. Peter paid that city a visit, probably not long after the council of Jerusalem. He had not lost the characteristics that marked him at an earlier day. He generally retained the intrepidity and fearlessness that he had exhibited in the Garden of Gethsemane; but at times he showed the timidity and vacillation of the palace-court, when he turned pale, swore, and fled at the questions of a girl. His conduct on this occasion in Antioch was marked by both these traits. Immediately on his arrival, acting in the spirit of Cæsarea and Jerusalem, he disregarded the Jewish traditions, and mingled freely with his Gentile brethren; but on the arrival from Jerusalem of some persons who are called "certain that came from James" he "withdrew and separated himself, fearing them which were of the circumcision." Paul declares that the other Jewish brethren acted a similar part, "insomuch that Barnabas also was carried away with their dissimulation."* But Paul stood firm, reproving Peter and asserting the rights of the Gentiles.†

Considerable portions of Paul's writings defy exposition unless the expositor keeps constantly in his hand the key furnished by this Hebrew-Gentile controversy. It showed itself in Corinth, and partly to settle it, partly to defend his apostolic authority, which had been assailed, Paul wrote his two letters to that church. It raised its hateful head in Colosse, and was the occasion of the Apostle's saying to the brethren there: "Let no man, therefore,

---

* Gal. ii: 12-13.

† The description, "certain that came from James," has given the commentators and historians much trouble, and various are the views regarding it. Some have explained it as meaning *certain which came from Jerusalem*, and others have regarded it as equivalent to *certain that gave themselves out as from James*. The language will not bear either refinement. Lightfoot supposes these persons "came invested with some power from James, which they abused." (Gal. ii: 12.) Alford takes a similar view. De Pressense thinks Paul and James did not understand the Jerusalem decree alike; holding that the latter, although advising that the Gentiles should not be required to keep the Law, never expected they would associate intimately with those who did. He says: "We can well imagine that he may have heard with alarm of the broad interpretation given at Antioch to his decision, and may have sent messengers from his church to put an end to an innovation which appeared to him at variance with the policy of conciliation of which he had been the wise promoter." (*Apostolic Era*, p. 140.) De Pressense, however, supposes that the messengers abused their powers.

judge you in meat, or in drink, or in respect of a holy day, or of the new moon, or of the Sabbath days."* It came up in Rome, and called out from Paul in his epistle a full statement of the doctrinal relations of the two religions. In the words of Alford:

"This epistle had for its end the settlement on the broad principles of God's truth and law, of the mutual relations and union in Christ, of God's ancient people and the recently engrafted world." Alford, therefore, appropriately calls it "an epistle to all the Gentiles from the Apostle of the Gentiles."†

In no other locality did the spread of the schismatical doctrine give the Apostle more distress of mind than in Galatia. He had planted the churches in this inland region; and so remote were they from Palestine and Palestinian influences, that he, perhaps, flattered himself that the disciples would here be left to form a normal type of Christianity undisturbed by factionists. If cherished, the hope was vain. The Galatians became "bewitched" by the Jewish zealots.‡ To correct the mischief that had been done in his absence, he wrote his famous Letter to the Galatian Churches, and if the Apostle ever tore a leaf out of the book of his own heart it was when he wrote this letter. It is doubtful whether even Paul ever crowded into the same compass so much personal incident, cogent argument, and pungent appeal. He entered upon the hortatory part of the epistle with the impatient cry: "Stand fast, therefore, in the liberty wherewith Christ hath made us free, and be not entangled again with the yoke of bondage."§ Whoever the author of the Epistle to the

---

* Col. ii: 16. † Introduction to Romans, iii: 5. ‡ Gal. iii: 1.

§ "The armory of this epistle has furnished their keenest weapons to the combatants in the two greatest controversies which in modern times have agitated the Christian Church; the one a struggle for liberty within the camp, the other a war of defense against assailants from without; the one vitally affecting the doctrine, the other the evidences of the Gos-

Hebrews may have been, he wrote the letter to prevent the Jewish Christians lapsing into pure Judaism. Paul's sense of the danger that threatened the Church, the depth and fervor of his own convictions, can be gathered from the strong language that he used in describing the Judaizers. He charged them with "perverting the Gospel,"* with preaching "another Gospel;"† he called those who demanded that Titus should be circumcised "false brethren, unawares brought in," and charged that they sought "to spy out" the liberty which the Gentile had in Christ.‡ Once more, he termed the Judaizers "dogs,"§ and declared that there were Jews who went to the extent of forbidding him "to speak to the Gentiles that they might be saved."‖

The citations given above show how wide spread, in the second half of the Apostolic Age, was the Jewish leaven. Still the fact calls for further elucidation.

The Jews of the Dispersion influenced the history of Christianity in two ways: they facilitated its early progress, and partially moulded the form that it assumed. In the first place, their presence in every community of considerable size offered to the evangelist or the apostle material to work upon similar to that found in Judea; a population that was already saturated with the great ideas of the Old Testament. In the second place, closely connected with these Jewish communities were a considerable number of Gentiles more or less thoroughly proselyted; while the sur-

---

pel.", (Lightfoot on "The Galatians," p. 67.) In the first of these cases, Luther chose this epistle as his most efficient weapon in attacking the corruptions of the Roman Church. The great reformer said: "The Epistle to the Galatians is my epistle; I have betrothed myself to it; it is my wife." In the second case, it was used by F. C. Bauer and his followers as the basis of their argument to prove that the earliest form of Christianity was only a modified Judaism.

*Gal. i: 7.   †II Cor. xi: 4.   ‡Gal. ii: 4.   §Phil. iii: 2.   ‖I Thes. ii: 16.

rounding Pagan society was to some extent leavened with Jewish ideas and modes of thought. On visiting a heathen city, Paul usually first sought out the synagogue and reasoned with his own countrymen "out of the Scriptures." As a consequence, the nucleus of almost all the Gentile churches was composed of Jews and proselytes. From these the Gospel passed by way of the partially leavened heathen to the pure idolators. In some instances the proselytes and Pagans gladly accepted the Gospel when the Hebrew refused it.* Now, the Jews of the Dispersion were generally much more catholic in thought and feeling than their Palestinian brethren, and were therefore prepared to take a more catholic view of the new faith. At the same time, they were Jews, largely under the influence of Jerusalem as well as of their traditional training. The first result was, that even in the Gentile churches the earliest conception of the Gospel had a strong Jewish coloring. The second result was a leverage for the zealots of Palestine, which they never would have found in a purely Gentile community. Still further, the Judaizers were not content to oppose the Pauline conception of the Gospel simply in Judea. A persistent and zealous propaganda appears to have been organized in Palestine, whose emissaries followed Paul into his chosen fields of labor, there to embarrass his action and destroy his influence. Probably the persons who came from James to Antioch belonged to this propaganda, and so, no doubt, did those who carried confusion and strife into the province of Galatia. These efforts at propagandism met with more success than, all things considered, we might have expected; as is shown by the impression they made on the fickle Galatians, as well as on communities where opinion and character were more stable. The Judaizers kept one object steadily in view: To un-

---

* Acts xiii: 44-49.

dermine the authority of Paul as an apostle. Here they had some advantages. Paul was not one of the Twelve; his conversion took place remote from Jerusalem; his relations with the Mother Church and with the Apostolic College were never intimate: all of which circumstances gave an opportunity, especially when he became the representative of an obnoxious doctrine, to discredit his work, sap the foundations of his authority, and even to deny the genuineness of his discipleship. The repeated and persistent denials of his apostleship are often referred to in his Epistles, and furnish the key to many passages in his writings. They called out, in the Letter to the Galatians, a full statement of the foundation of his authority, and of his relations to the Apostles of the Circumcision. In view of these incessant attacks it is nothing strange that the Apostle, writing to the Corinthians, should have crowned his recital of the "perils" which he had encountered during his ministry with, "In perils among false brethren."*

How the Jewish leaven worked in a Gentile church—how it embarrassed the Apostle, and conditioned both his preaching and his Epistles—can best be shown, perhaps, by looking into the Church of Corinth.

Paul was the founder of that church. He planted it in his first missionary journey in Europe; the journey in which he visited Philippi, Thessalonica, Amphipolis, Berea, and Athens—the scenes of the first missionary work in Europe with the probable exception of Rome. In Corinth he found the Jew Aquila and Priscilla his wife, with whom he abode and wrought at his craft of tent making. There he found Justus, Crispus, Gaius, and Erastus the chamberlain; there he reasoned in the synagogue every Sabbath and persuaded the Jews and Greeks; there he encountered the hostility of the Jews and the indifference of

---

* II Cor. xi: 26.

Gallio the deputy: nevertheless "he continued a year and six months preaching the word of God among them."

The history of this first evangelical labor in Corinth is given with some minuteness in Chapter XVIII of the Acts. In his two Epistles to the Corinthians, the Apostle often speaks of his relation to that church, "I have planted." Again: "For though you have ten thousand instructors in Christ, yet have ye not many fathers, for in Christ Jesus I have begotten you through the Gospel." Once more:

"When I came to you, I came not with excellency of speech or of wisdom, declaring unto you the testimony of God. For I determined not to know anything among you, save Jesus Christ and Him crucified. And I was with you in weakness, and in fear, and in much trembling. And my speech and my preaching was not with enticing words of man's wisdom, but in demonstration of the Spirit and of power. That your faith should not stand in the wisdom of men, but in the power of God."*

But Paul's zeal in the Gospel, and his honorable delicacy of feeling about building on other men's foundations—two motive powers that constantly kept him on the frontier of Christianity, or far within the dominions of heathenism—did not secure him against persisted and powerful attacks. No sooner, therefore, had he, in obedience to the Macedonian cry, crossed the sea and made the circuit of the principal cities of Greece, than the emissaries of the Palestinian propaganda followed upon his track. At least they appeared in Antioch, and attempted to give a Jewish rendition of the Gospel. Nothing more was wanting to introduce into that Church, deeply marked as it was by the fickle temper and unbridled manners of the city, those "contentions" of which we read in the first Letter to the Corinthians. Every one said, "I am of Paul, and I of Apollos, and I of Cephas;" while even the sacred name of Christ was used for partizan and schismatical purposes. As the great name of Paul stood in the way of the Juda-

---

* I Cor. ii: 1-5.

izers, his authority must be destroyed. Accordingly, they impugned his motives, calumniated his character, and denied his apostleship. To support this denial, two arguments seem to have been urged. *First,* It was affirmed that Paul had no personal knowledge of the Saviour, in fact, that he had never seen him. *Second,* It was affirmed that his not claiming remuneration for his services in Corinth was a confession of weakness and want of authority. This argument ran, "If Paul is an apostle why does he not act like an apostle—demand support for himself and a sister that he leads about as his wife?" That these arguments made a considerable impression on the minds of the Corinthians, although Paul was their father in the Gospel, no one who has read the Epistles can doubt. In fact, to reply to them, to assert his authority, and thereby to protect the little flock that he had gathered, was a leading purpose in writing them. It had become a solemn duty to speak. Not to do so would be a confession of imposture, to suffer the Lord's banner to be trailed in the dust without protest, and probably to see the foundation that he had laid in prayers and in tears ground to powder and scattered to the four winds of heaven. He *must* speak. Hence the cogent argument, the indignant remonstrance, and the tender expostulation with which he addresses his children in the faith.

We are now in possession of the key to a large part of the First Corinthians. Paul asks, "Am I not an apostle? Am I not free? Have I not seen Jesus Christ our Lord? Are not ye my work in the Lord?" He declares: "If I am not an apostle unto others, yet doubtless I am to you; for the seal of my apostleship are ye in the Lord." Coming to the charge that his unpaid teaching witnessed against him, he says:

"Mine answer to them that do examine me in this: Have we not power to eat and to drink? Have we not power to lead about a sister, a wife, as well as other apostles, and as the brethren of the Lord and Cephas? Or I only and Barnabas, have not we power to forbear working? Who goeth a warfare any time at his own charges? who planteth a vineyard and eateth not of the fruit thereof? or who feedeth a flock, and eateth not of the milk of the flock?" He quotes the law of Moses: "Thou shalt not muzzle the mouth of the ox that treadeth out the corn." He clenches the argument by referring to the Temple service: "They which wait at the altar are partakers with the altar."*

He sums up by declaring: "Even so hath the Lord ordained that they which preach the Gospel should live of the Gospel."

Thus far the argument is all on the side of those who "did examine" Paul. But, having fixed immovably this bulwark of the Church, the right of the ministry to a support, he turns to vindicate his own conduct. Never was vindication more complete! Never defense more honorable to its author!"

"Nevertheless we have not used this power; but suffer all things, lest we should hinder the Gospel of Christ."

And again:

"But I have used none of these things; neither have I written these things that it should be so done unto me: for it were better for me to die than that any man should make my glorying void."

The way is now fully prepared for the grand climax:

"For though I preach the Gospel"—that is, without pay, "mine own hands ministering unto my necessities,"—"for though I preach the Gospel, I have nothing to glory of: for necessity is laid upon me; yea, woe is unto me if I preach not the Gospel."

In another form the argument is this: "I could rightly have claimed compensation in Corinth; I refused to ask or receive it, lest the Gospel should be hindered; but I am entitled to no credit or praise on that account. I have nothing to glory of. This work was laid upon my hands and my heart without my choice; it is my Master's, and I

---

* I Cor. ix: 1-13.

have not option in the premises." Here is the spring of that mighty spirit—the secret of that mighty life! "I am not my own;" "I am bought with a price;" "necessity is laid upon me;" "woe is unto me if I preach not the Gospel."

Having thus asserted the power *under* which he wrought, he next asserts the rule *according* to which he wrought:

> "For though I be free from all men, yet have I made myself servant unto all, that I might gain the more. And unto the Jews I became as a Jew, that I might gain the Jews; to them that are under the Law, as under the Law, that I might gain them that are under the Law; to them that are without Law, as without Law, (being not without law to God, but under the law to Christ,) that I might gain them that are without Law. To the weak became I as weak, that I might gain the weak. I am made all things to all men, that I might by all means save some."*

For the statement of this great law of Christian action, we are indebted to the Jewish-Gentile conflict.

Among the Gentiles, Paul kept the banner of catholic Christianity full high advanced. By ceaseless effort and watching, he thwarted both the Palestinian propaganda and the local zealots, in their efforts to Judaize the Gentile Christians. He impressed on the Gentile Church, which continually expanded under care, his own conception of the Gospel. But his relations with Judea became yearly more and more unsatisfactory. His unbelieving countrymen hated him with a peculiar hatred. This was partly because they regarded him as the foremost apostate, and partly because he fraternized with the heathen, which was counted not only irreligious but unpatriotic. Still further, his relations to the Palestinian Church were very precarious. When he first visited Jerusalem after his conversion, he was an object of suspicion to the disciples, and it was only through the friendly mediation of Barnabas that the feeling was removed. Although allayed for the time being, the

---

* I Cor. ix: 19-22.

feeling of hostility broke out again in a new form. If it was less general, it was more intense. The Apostle labored chiefly in fields remote from Palestine. He rarely visited Jerusalem. He was almost a stranger to the Mother Church. Probably his Epistles did not circulate in Judea. His enemies circulated false and exaggerated reports of his teaching. He was represented as a reviler of Moses and a seducer of the Jews. The Palestinian disciples had expected that Jerusalem would continue to be the heart of Christendom; and now, that they saw the supremacy likely to pass to the Gentiles, the more bigoted and fanatical hated the agent by which that end was effected. The feeling manufactured in Judea found its way to the centres of Paul's ministry, and became an obstacle in his path. His position became unbearable to him. He determined, if possible, to come to an understanding with the Palestinian Church. Postponing his long projected visit to Rome, he at last turned his face once more toward Jerusalem, determined, if possible, to put an end to the alienation of feeling. He had an additional reason for going in his desire to carry in person the fund collected in Achaia and Macedonia for the poor in Palestine. He could no longer endure a condition of things that had distressed his heart and embarrassed his work. It is evident that he looked forward to the visit with many forebodings. He asked the prayers of the brethren in Rome, that he might be delivered from them that were unbelievers in Judea, and that his ministration which was for Jerusalem might prove acceptable to the saints;* a passage which shows that he feared the bounty he had gathered would be refused. At different places on the way he gave expression to his solicitude. He said to the elders of Ephesus:

---

*Rom. xv: 31.

THE MINISTRY OF PAUL. 91

"Behold, I go bound in the spirit unto Jerusalem, not knowing the things that shall befall me there; save that the Holy Ghost witnesseth in every city, saying that bonds and afflictions abide me."*

At Cæsarea, a determined effort was made by those who intimately knew the feeling in Judea to induce him to abandon his purpose, but without effect.† He declared his willingness to die in Jerusalem for the sake of the Lord Jesus, showing that his visit, in his own estimation, was a high religious mission. On the day of his arrival in the city, he was cordially received by some of the brethren, and not less cordially the next day by James and the Elders. At the same time his presence gave rise, in the minds of the latter, to much anxiety. They promptly called his attention to his danger, and, strange as it may seem, connected it with the very greatness of the Palestinian Church. In the very breath that they glorified the Lord for the things He had wrought among the Gentiles by Paul's ministry, they said unto him:

"Thou seest, brother, how many thousands of Jews there are which believe; and they are all zealous of the Law: and they are informed of thee, that thou teachest all the Jews which are among the Gentiles to forsake Moses, saying, that they ought not to circumcise their children, neither to walk after the customs. What is it, therefore? The multitude must needs come together: for they will hear that thou art come."‡

They concluded by advising him to perform, in company with four others, whose expenses he should pay, the vow of the Nazarite, to convince the Jews that he walked orderly and kept the Law. The results of this attempt to propitiate a fanatical multitude, need not be here recited. It is enough to remark, that the Mother Church had become large; that "the thousands of Jews" who believed were still largely Jewish in feeling and tone; that the hostility to Paul was so strong that his very presence was the signal for an out-break; and that his danger, in the esti-

---

*Acts xx: 22-3.   † *Ibid.* xxi: 12-13.   ‡ *Ibid.* xxi: 20-22.

mation of James and the Elders, had its chief source among the more fanatical members of the Church. It is evident, too, that he had his friends, the brethren who received him gladly, as well as James and the Elders. The actual relations of the Judaizers to the events which led to his arrest and imprisonment, are not clear. Some scholars think the unbelievers of Romans xv: 31, were "Hebrew" Christians; it is certain that the dreaded "multitude" of Acts xxi: 22, were such; and there is nothing violent in the view taken by some good authorities, 'that the Asiatic Jews " who stirred up all the people" belonged to the same class. Nor is there anything unreasonable in the supposition, that members of the Jerusalem Church, to whose necessities the Gentile Christians under Paul's direction had often ministered, joined with unbelieving Jews in the onset that cost the Apostle his liberty, and finally his life.

Justice to Paul's teaching demands that one thing more be added. He was not harsh towards his Jewish brethren, nor is there any evidence to show that he taught the Jews of the Dispersion to abandon the Mosaic rites. He was perfectly willing the Jewish disciples should observe the old ritual if they saw fit, though he did not fail to point out the superiority of grace and faith to the works of the Law. The key-note of his teaching was: "In Christ Jesus neither circumcision availeth anything nor uncircumcision; but faith which worketh by love."* To conciliate his "Hebrew" brethren, he was willing to go to the farthest verge of charity. He accommodated himself to their prejudices, so long as the accommodation involved no surrender of principle. He circumcised Timothy "because of the Jews which were in those quarters",† as a prudential measure; but when, under different circumstances, it was demanded that Titus should be subjected to the same rite, he "gave place

---

* Gal. v: 6.   † Acts xvi: 3.

by subjection, no, not for an hour."* He visited all kinds of communities, mingled with all sorts of people, and his desire neither to "run nor labor in vain" called for the greatest wisdom in teaching and the highest prudence in conduct. He probably observed the Law himself, though he no doubt saw that it would by-and-by wholly pass away. It was in the midst of this fierce Judeo-Gentile conflict that, under the guidance of the Divine Spirit, he applied the Christian Law to some most difficult and perplexing questions of casuistry. In the midst of the same controversy, he laid the foundation of the only enduring theology—the theology that discriminates between principle and faith on the one hand, and expediency and opinion on the other. Distressing as was the division, it was not without its compensation; since it gave the Church some of the most valuable and admirable of the Apostle's writings.

It remains to look at the Church in this age more closely. Borrowing some current terms from French politics, it may be said to have consisted of a center, a right, and a left. The center was composed of the moderates, all Jews, who began with supposing that the Gentiles were to come into the Gospel by way of Judaism, but who were gradually led to welcome them into the fellowship without circumcision. They zealously kept the Law themselves, in a ceremonial sense were as much Jews as ever, and would have regarded it as a departure from duty for a Jewish Christian to do or be otherwise. But they were willing to leave the Gentiles free, except as they were bound by the prohibitions of the Jerusalem decree. On this platform stood the Apostles of the Circumcision, who differed among themselves somewhat in their peculiar apprehensions of the truth. The right was composed of the Judaizers, determined, fanatical, protesting against the new departure as subverting both the Law and the

---

* Gal. ii: 3-5.

doctrine of Christ. What their conception of the Gospel was, has already appeared. They rested on the center because there they found the ritual observed, and also a measure of sympathy. They constantly asserted that they represented the views and feelings of the Church at Jerusalem. Especially did they claim the sanction of the Apostle James. The left was made up of the great mass of the Gentiles and the Hellenists, together with a few "Hebrews" who had broken away from their more conservative brethren. This was the progressive section of the church. There were no material doctrinal differences between the center and the left, though there were differences in culture, tone, and of opinion; while the right was so Levitical in its construction of the Gospel as scarcely to be entitled to the name Christian.

The relative size of the three sections can be determined only approximately. Outside of Palestine, the left was plainly in the ascendency; but inside, which was more powerful, the center or the right? Beyond Jérusalem it is impossible to tell with certainty, though there is some reason to think with De Pressensè, that the Judaizing form of Christianity assumed a more decided character in the small towns than at the Capital. But in the Holy City there need be no controversy over this question, and there can be none among those who refrain from *a priori* construction, and accept as final the only historical account that has been preserved. Here the center firmly held the ground. This is shown by the history of the Jerusalem Council. What was there done—the sending of Judas and Silas to Antioch, the repudiation of the men who had troubled the brethren in that city, "subverting their souls," together with the compromise—was done by the whole church, and not simply by the Apostles and Elders.* Nor is there any

---

* Acts xv: 22.

evidence to show that the Mother Church ever shifted her ground either to the right or the left. At the time of Paul's last visit, it was not the Judaizers only that gave him trouble. The description: "They are all zealous of the Law; and they are all informed of thee, that thou teachest all the Jews which are among the Gentiles to forsake Moses, saying, that they ought not to circumcise their children, neither to walk after the customs," applied to the great body of the church, including the center, who were misinformed, as well as the right, who were inflamed with undying hostility. The treatment meted out to Paul does not prove that the Mother Church was controlled by the zealots, but it does prove the strong Judaic tone of the disciples in Jerusalem. As compared with the center and the left, the Judaizers were few in number. Their constant activity and intense bitterness, are well calculated to cause us to exaggerate their numbers and importance. But whatever their relative numerical and moral strength, these three classes, though they tend to shade into each other, are easily distinguishable. The lines separating them were produced into the next age, as I now hasten to show.

IX.—THE CATASTROPHE.

The history of the Jewish-Christian Church opened most auspiciously. How gloriously the work of evangelization began on Pentecost! How gloriously it went on for a whole generation! A few passages in the Acts show this most conclusively. "And the same day there was added unto them about three thousand souls."* "The Lord added to

---

* Acts ii: 41.

the Church daily such as should be saved.* A little later, "the number of men was about five thousand."† "And believers were the more added unto the Lord; multitudes both of men and women."‡ "A great company of the priests were obedient to the faith."§ At the time of Paul's last visit to Jerusalem, in the year 58, the believing Jews were counted by thousands (literally "myriads," or tens of thousands). Such progress was quite as encouraging as the contemporaneous growth of the Gentile Church; and it seemed to give promise that the Jews would ultimately become a Christian nation. But this promise was most delusive; for, although Jerusalem continued the heart of the Church until its fall, from that time onward Jewish Christianity fell into a hopeless decay. The principal causes will appear as we go on with the history.

The fall of Jerusalem came in the year 70, just at the close of the Apostolic Age. It was a blow from which neither Judea nor the Palestinian Church ever recovered. What Jewish Christianity might have been had not Palestine suffered the terrible vengeance of the Roman arms, it is idle to conjecture; but it is certain that war and political commotions had a powerful influence over its post-Apostolic history. The Christian Jews were now more completely separated from their unbelieving countrymen. Even the Romans ceased to regard them as a Jewish sect. The Christians denounced their unconverted brethren as the cause of the woes that had fallen upon their common country; while the latter retorted the charge with a double bitterness. Anticipating the impending blow, the great majority of disciples in Jerusalem withdrew from the city, refusing, as Lightfoot puts it, "to share the fate of their countrymen." They declared by an overt act that henceforth "they were strangers, that now at length, their

---

* Acts ii: 47.   † *Ibid.* iv: 4.   ‡ *Ibid.* v: 14.   § *Ibid.* vi: 7.

hopes and interests were separate."* This intensification of feeling almost closed the door to further evangelization among the Palestinian Jews. Over and above this obstacle, the agitated state of society rendered the growth of the Church an impossibility. On the one hand, less evangelical labor was done; on the other, what was done was to but little purpose. Besides, the disappearance of the Apostles of the Circumcision, who had been the pillars of the Mother Church, and the want of men able to take their places, powerfully contributed to the same end. What is more, sharp, persistent opposition thinned the ranks of the feebler members, while the calamities that overtook the Christians in common with their countrymen, by showing that their new religion did not bring exemption from temporal ills, drove some of the less resolute back into the ranks of orthodox Judaism. These causes conspired materially to waste the strength of the Palestinian Church from the year 70 onward.

But it is time to inquire what effects these events had on the Jewish type of Christian character and doctrine. From one point of view, we might expect that it would have been favorable. The chastisement of the nation, the desecration of the national sanctuary, the razing of Jerusalem, would turn the minds of the Palestinian Christians from legal observances to the heart of the Gospel; thus weaning them from the altar and the Law. Their greater separation from the body of their people would also tend in the same direction. Properly guided, the Jewish Christians might have found a school of Providence in their very calamities; but the great teachers who had "reasoned with them out of the Scriptures," had passed away, and they were left without the needed guidance. Instead of expanding and softening, the Jewish heart petrified under

---

* On Galatians, p. 303.

its sorrows; the Jewish mind, instead of becoming more catholic, became narrower than ever. In fact, the points in which the Jewish Christians were most lacking, were not those most likely to be brought out by affliction. Under more propitious circumstances, they might have cast off the bias imposed upon them by their Judaism; but, as has often been the case under similar circumstances, calamity froze the current of their sympathies and confirmed them in their narrow creed. It is not meant that this was true of all, as will appear in the following paragraphs.

The Christians of Jerusalem did not sympathize with the revolt that brought upon Judea the vengeance of the Romans, and they were disposed to escape its consequences. Remembering the prophetic warnings of their Master, the great body of them withdrew to Pella, a city of Decapolis, east of the Jordan. Here the church was re-formed. At a later day this community is said to have returned to Jerusalem, there to rebuild the Christian Zion, as the captives from Babylon rebuilt the Jewish Zion many centuries before. It is certain that there was a second church of "Hebrew" proclivities in Jerusalem. This church was soon scattered, and forever. Towards the middle of the second century, under the leadership of Barcocheba, "the son of a star," the Jews once more broke out into rebellion. This was put down in the thorough-going way of which the Romans were such consummate masters. To make all future insurrections impossible, the Emperor Hadrian fortified the city, which had been partially rebuilt, made it a Roman colony, gave it the name Ælia Capitolina, and issued a decree forbidding a Jew to approach it under pain of death. A Jewish-Christian church in Jerusalem now became an impossibility. No Jew could live in the Roman city, unless he renounced the Law, and ceased to be a Jew in every sense except the physical. As many of the Christians as could not comply with the conditions of residence, returned to Pella, where it is probable a considerable part of the original community had remained. Since their departure no Christian Church of "Hebrew" tendencies has ever worshipped the God of their fathers in the City of David. According to Neander, there are traces of a church in Pella that practised circumcision, as late as the fifth century.* Its history, however, is involved in much obscurity. After its disappearance we find no trace in history of a Jewish-Christian Church anywhere.

But we are not to suppose that the harsh measures of Hadrian banished Christianity from Judea, or even from Jerusalem. While Jews were strictly excluded from Ælia Capitolina, Christians were welcome to reside there. A new church arose on the ruins of the old one, composed mostly of Gentiles, and of thoroughly Gentile tone. A Jew could belong to it only by renouncing Judaism; a condition with which no one of the Apostles, unless it were Paul, would have been willing to comply. This resulted from no ecclesiastical arrangement, but from the law regulating residence. The breach between catholic Christianity and "Hebrew" Christianity continued to widen; the former, once planted in Judea, spread more and more, while the latter assumed a definitely heretical form. How large a part of the original Palestinian Church renounced their Judaism and stood with the catholic Christians, and how large a part fell into heresy, it is impossible to tell. It is safe to say that the more liberal section, those that above I have called the left—perhaps I had better say the spiritual descendants of these—abandoned everything that was distinctive of Jewish Christianity, and became affiliated with their Gentile brethren. How far these were reinforced from the moderates, or the center, we have no means of determining. At this point the stream

---

*Hist. of the Chr. Religion, vol. I. p. 344.

divides. Those Jewish Christians who abandoned Judaism lost their identity by being merged with the great body of the catholic Church; while those who persisted in being Jews, were accounted heretical, and with the fifth century they disappeared. Thus, Jewish Christianity lived longer in heresy than in orthodoxy. Dr. Schaff says from the conversion of Cornelius "the narrow Judaism which made circumcision the condition of salvation, became henceforth a formal heresy."* A "formal heresy" this narrow Judaism certainly became, but I cannot think it was generally so regarded until a later date, when the catholic consciousness had become more fully developed.

It remains rapidly to trace the history of the various Judeo-Christian sects.

In the second century, we meet a very grossly heretical form of Jewish Christianity. This is Ebionitism. The name of these heretics, as well as their doctrine, has been the subject of much controversy. But it seems to be conclusively shown that the name was from a Hebrew word meaning "poor." According to Uhlhorn, three steps can be made out in its history.

(1.) "It can hardly be questioned," he says, "that this name, like Nazareans, designated all Christians, because they themselves were poor, and because poverty had so deep a significance under the Gospel." (2.) "The name also being of Hebrew derivation came to be the special designation of Jewish Christians." (3.) "And when Jewish Christianity, outstripped by the Gentile Church, separated itself heretically, whilst Christians of Jewish origin who fell in with the Gentile development became fully identified with this, the name Ebionites came to be the general designation of heretical Judaizing Christianity."†

He adds that in the second sense, the name is older than the sect; but in the third sense the sect is older than the name.

Ebionitism is a generic name for a medley of strange

---

* Apostolic Ch. p. 223.
† Herzog's *Real Encyclopedia*, Art. "Ebionites."

doctrines. Dr. Schaff describes it as having been a "Judaizing, psuedo-Petrine Christianity, or, as it may equally well be called, a Christianizing Judaism."* He further describes it as a "particularistic construction of the Christian religion," a "gross realism and literalism." In but one important particular was it an advance from Judaism. Its adherents accepted Jesus as the Messiah, but under such limitations as to rob Him of most of His dignities and powers. The Ebionites generally denied His supernatural birth. In other words, they saw in Jesus little more than the realization of the vulgar Messianic ideas entertained by the Jews at the time of Christ's coming. They held the Law of Moses to be universally and perpetually valid, and circumcision as universal a rite as baptism. They regarded the Gentile Christians as apostates, and looked upon the Apostle Paul with undying hatred. Historians generally recognize two types of Ebionitism: one, represented by the vulgar Ebionites, was of a strictly legal or Levitical character; the other was of a speculative and mystical nature, and prepared the way for Gnosticism. The first was a cross of Christianity and Pharisaism; the second of Christianity and Essenism. The religious paternity of both branches is found in the New Testament. In the words of Lightfoot:

"If the Pharisaic Ebionites are the direct lineal descendants of the false brethren who seduced St. Paul's Galatian converts from their allegiance, the Essene Ebionites bear a striking family likeness to those Judaizers against whom he raises his voice as endangering the safety of the Church at Colossae."†

The Ebionites produced an extensive literature. They were found in Decapolis, in Asia Minor, in Palestine, in Cyprus, and in all the great centers of the Empire. At the close of the second century, they were so formidable a

---

*Hist. Church, vol. I. p. 211. †On Galatians, p. 313.

sect as to call out a formal refutation from Irenæus.* But a century later they had spent their force.

Another body of Jewish sectaries were the Nazareans, a name once applied to all Christians, but now become a sect-appellation. They sprang from the center or moderate portion of the Apostolic Church, and stood firmly on the platform of the Jerusalem compromise. They did not share the feeling of the Ebionites toward the Gentiles and the Apostle Paul. They regretted the violence and grossness of their more heretical brethren. They rigorously kept the law of Moses themselves, and held that all Jews should do so, but did not seek to impose it upon the Gentile Christians. There seems to be no reason for calling them heretics, except that they continued to stand on the decree of the Apostolic Council when the time had come for abandoning it. "Stunted, separatist Christians of the school of James," is Dr. Schaff's description of them. Jerome says: "Wishing to be both Jews and Christians, they were neither the one nor the other." The Nazareans sank to an insignificant sect, and early disappeared.

A summary of the principal points covered by this history is reserved for the next section, but two or three observations on the facts presented in the present section are called for:

1. The Jewish Christian has no place among the creators of Christian theology. He lacked the scientific qualities necessary for the requisite analytical insight and philosophical construction. The Jew could be an intense, wrapt seer, but not a philosopher. Besides, the Palestinian Church had passed into the period of her decline before the theological period fairly began. At the same time, however, the Christian Jew exercised a powerful negative influence over the development of theological doctrines.

---

* Against Heresies.

The gross materialistic Ebionitism of some, as well as the transcendental Gnosticism of others, hastened the day of formal creeds, and largely determined the character of those first crystalizations of theological opinions known as the earliest symbols of the Church.

2. Ebionitism and its affiliated isms were unmistakable heresies. The Gospel gives large play to individuality: it is not a bed of Procrustes. Even the Apostles, in setting it forth, preserved all their personal traits. Hold what theory of inspiration one may, he cannot deny that Paul's apprehension of Christianity is not Peter's, nor James's, nor John's. But these different conceptions are not contradictory; they do not exclude each other. But no stretch of Christian liberality can bring the Ebionitism of the second century and the catholic conception of Christianity under the same species; they do exclude each other.

3. The Jewish-Christian Church is at once an instructive and awful spectacle. It is a most impressive warning to the people of God. Before the fall of Jerusalem it could no longer have been a question, with a discerning man, what the tone of Historic Christianity was to be. The Gentile field was broad, the Palestinian narrow. Gentile Christianity was full of the elements of life and growth. Jewish Christianity, promising as was its beginning, was early smitten with sterility. The one was catholic, the other particular. One grew, the other withered. Unlike Gentile Christianity, Jewish had no power to purify and renew itself. The other great peoples of antiquity, as the Greeks and Latins, left behind them National Churches which have survived to this day; but there is no Jewish-Christian Church. The epitaph of Judaism is the epitaph of Jewish Christianity: "YOUR HOUSE IS LEFT UNTO YOU DESOLATE." The causes of decay in both cases were much the same. Assigning all due importance to political facts, the great moral cause was the Levitical tendency.

There could be but one Moses, one Book of Leviticus, one group of Rabbis. Unfortunately, however, the Levitical conception of the Gospel did not pass away with the Palestinian Church. The spirit that turned both Judaism and Jewish Christianity into petrifactions, surviving both Jerusalem and Pella, has continually passed into new forms. It is the presiding genius of Romanism. It haunts many of the sanctuaries of Protestantism. It changes its doctrinal tests from age to age, and proposes new conditions of fellowship; but in itself it changes not; it is the same that it was when it led the great body of the Jews to reject Christ, and caused so many of those who did ostensibly accept him either to fall back into Judaism or to lapse into heresy. De Pressense is quite right when he says: "Judeo-Christianity was not so much a simple fact, as the embodiment of a principle, and natural tendency of the human heart."*

X.—SUMMARY AND CONCLUSION.

Perhaps it will be a service to the reader to sum up the argument.

1. *Introduction.*—The field of Christian Dogmatics is mapped out; the parts played in theological creation by Greece, Rome, and Germany are assigned to them, and the influence of Judea on doctrinal development is pointed out.

2. *Before Pentecost.*—Jesus's affiliation with the Jews is mentioned; the promised restoration and the Messianic predictions are quoted, and the question, How did the Jews construe these scriptures? discussed at some length.

---

*Early Years of Christianity, N. Y., 1871, p. 217.

An attempt is also made to determine, from a Jewish standpoint, the relations of Jews and Gentiles in Messiah's Kingdom. Especially is it attempted to determine what was the religious consciousness of the disciples just previous to the Pentecost.

3. *Jerusalem and Judea* are next considered—the influence of Pentecost on the Christian mind; the introduction into the Church of the Hellenistic element; the beginning of the Hebrew-Grecian controversy, and the preaching of Stephen.

4. *Samaria.*—Under this head, the history of Phillip's preaching in one of the cities of that province is related; and the bearing of the Samaritan conversions on the Church at Jerusalem considered. The section closes with the Eunuch's conversion on the road to Gaza.

5. *The Conversion of Cornelius.*—Here are noticed the slow growth of the Apostle Peter's mind; his receiving the Centurion and his kinsmen into the Church; the furor that was raised over it at Jerusalem; and, particularly, the bearings on the history of the Church of what had been done in Cæsarea.

6. *The Conversion of Greeks in Antioch.*—Some features of the city are noticed; the relations of Antioch to Samaria and Cæsarea are pointed out; the first preaching in the city, including the conversion of Greeks, and the labors of Barnabas and Saul are sketched.

7. *The Council of Jerusalem.*—Here it is shown how the teaching of "certain men which came down from Judea" introduced the Jewish-Gentile question into the Church at Corinth; how the question was referred to the Apostles and Elders at Jerusalem; and how it was decided, for the time, by refusing to lay the Mosaic yoke on the necks of the Gentiles, and by commanding them to abstain from pollutions to idols, from fornication, from things

strangled, and from blood. The section closes with a number of inferences from the narrative.

8. *The Ministry of Paul.*—Here the great work of the Apostle to the Gentiles is described. He is shown in strenuous antagonism to the Judaizing element; attention is called to the notes of the Jewish-Gentile controversy constantly heard in his Epistles; and the purpose, progress, and end of his last visit to Jerusalem is stated.

9. Last of all, the *Catastrophe of the Jewish-Christian Church* is told. The destruction of Jerusalem; the foundation of Pella; the final separation of the Palestinian Church into the catholic element and the several heretical elements, the absorption of the former into the Church Catholic, and the final disappearance of the latter from history.

In so broad a generalization as I have sketched, there is abundant room for errors of detail. Some, I am aware, will deny the correctness of my construction, as a whole. But to me, after long and patient study, it accords with the facts of human nature, with what we know of Jewish culture, and harmonizes all parts of the inspired history. Unless I am mistaken, the common opinion is, that catholic Christianity appears in the very beginning of the evangelical narrative. So, indeed, it does in the utterances of Christ; but to hold that the disciples, the Apostles even, understood the Gospel in its wide bearings, at the ascension of the Master, or on Pentecost, as they did twenty years later, is to set at nought both the laws of the human mind and the facts of history. Partly to correct that conception, I have sought to show what kind of a Messiah the Jews expected; what Jesus taught as to the nature and extent of His reign; how his disciples understood Him; how the Jewish consciousness was unfolded into the Jewish-Christian, and this, again, into the catholic-Christian. I have sought to exhibit the divine and the human elements in their proper relations, paying especial attention to the latter because they are so frequently overlooked. If my interpretation and synthesis of the facts be correct, then God wrought in the Early Church in accordance with a general principle. Universalism did not at once take the place of particularism. Christ taught a world-embracing Gospel, but a generation passed before the Church grasped its full import. The leaven gradually leavened the lump. New inspirations were poured into the souls of men, as they expanded to receive them. "The earth brings forth fruits of herself: first the blade, then the ear, after that the full corn in the ear." Such is the divine law, in nature and in grace.

NOTE.

F. C. BAUER'S THEORIES.

The most thorough discussion in the recent history of Church literature, turns on the nature of the original Christianity and its early history. It had long been held by the Socinians that this Christianity was pure Ebionitism, and that the doctrines of the divinity of Christ and the sacrificial atonement, sprang up after the New Testament had been completed. In the hands of the Socinians, this plea never made much impression on the Christian world; but in the present century it has been caught up by other hands, and been made the centre of the most formidable line of battle arrayed in recent times against catholic Christianity.

F. C. Bauer, who has marshalled this line of battle, was born in 1792, and at the age of thirty-four he was made professor of evangelical theology at the university of Tübingen. He was a man of a subtle and profound intellect, and of immense learning. He invented a new method of dealing with Church history, propounded a new theory of the rise and spread of the so-called catholic faith. In other words, he was the author of the Tübingen School of Dogmatics and Church History; a school that varies somewhat widely in its teaching on minor points, but that holds firmly to the same leading propositions. Christlieb says Bauer's name "will remain inscribed in the history of modern theology, when that of many others now known to every one, will long since have been effaced." He further says: "Bauer was one of the greatest, if not the greatest, theological scholar of this century," "the most notable historian of the Church and her doctrines after the death of Neander," "the most indefatigable of investigators," "head and shoulders above all other opponents of the miraculous."* Bauer's leading views may be rapidly stated as follows: He builds on the foundation of Hegelian Pantheism,

---

* Modern Doubt and Christian Belief. N. Y. 1874, pp. 505.

setting aside the supernatural as an impossibility, at war with "historical connection." Having thus stripped Christianity of every shred of supernaturalism, but for philosophical rather than historical reasons, he refers its origin and growth to purely human causes.

Its genesis is explained through its connection with Heathenism and Judaism. The universalism of Christianity, one of its marked features, had its type in the political universalism of the Roman empire. "Christianity stood upon the same level to which the Roman state had raised itself, by its world-wide monarchy."

The purely moral character of its facts and doctrines, another striking aspect, was furnished by the pervasive Greek philosophy. But the chief force in the evolution of Christianity was Judaism—Christianity is Judaism spiritualized. Here Bauer's reasoning must be more closely followed.

The Jews expected a Messiah; not a suffering and redeeming Saviour, but a prophet-king. Jesus thought Himself this Messiah, and His followers so regarded Him. The latter, however, saw in Him nothing more than a realization of the current Messianic expectations of the Jews; they never thought of clothing Jesus with Divine attributes. Accordingly, they differed from their unbelieving countrymen only in this: they accepted Jesus as the Messiah—a teacher and ruler sent from God — while the latter did not so accept Him. They fell far below the level of their Master's universalism. Salvation must be sought in the Jewish Church; circumcision was indispensable to discipleship; the Law was of perpetual and universal validity. In short, the Ebionitism of the second century was the primitive Christianity. At an early day, however, Paul appeared, preaching that the Gospel was a universal religion, and that the Gentiles might embrace it without coming under the yoke of the Jewish rites. The Apostles of the Circumcision opposed this new conception of the faith. Hence arose a controversy that split the Church into two factions—a Petrine faction, that held to a Jewish Gospel; and a Pauline faction, that held to a Gentile Gospel. So far, therefore, from Ebionitism being a heresy, the catholic Christianity was the real departure from the original faith. When the Apostolic Age had passed away, an effort was made to reconcile the two schools. Only five books of the New Testament are genuine—the Epistles to the Romans, to the Corinthians, and to the Galatians, written by Paul, and Revelation, written by John.

No book that contains fully developed the doctrine of Christ's divinity is earlier than the second century; for even Paul had no such high conception of His character. All the books of the New Testament were written for one or two purposes—to advocate the peculiar view of a school, or to effect a compromise between the schools. In the Tübingen nomenclature, the former are called "tendency writings." Galatians, for example, has a Gentile "tendency," and Revelation a Hebrew "tendency."

The older the writing, the less trace of "tendency," and the more trustworthy the book. Matthew is the most authentic of the Gospels; Luke has a Pauline "tendency;" Mark is mediatory; and John was not written until the second century. The Acts is an ingenious attempt to conceal the controversy between Peter and Paul, and was written in the interest of compromise. Bauer fully agrees with the old Socinians, in holding that the primitive Christianity was unitarian, but he differs from them in finding plain trace of the doctrine of Christ's divinity in the first century.

It will be seen that Baur repudiates the generally received account of the catholic Christianity, and denies that the New Testament is a veracious history. Holding, as he did, that the early history of the Church was unwritten, he undertook, in his various historical writings, to construct one that should be worthy of credence. For this purpose, he employed his theory of history, first analyzing the various human forces acting in the East at the opening of our era, and then deducing probable effects from them. He then seized hold of various facts emphasized in the preceding naratives. He laid stress on the gross Messianic ideas of the Jews; the "Hebrew" bias of the early Disciples; the late introduction into the Church of the Gentiles, and the commotion produced by their reception; the Council of Jerusalem; the wide-spread controversy about the Jewish rites; and the existence of the Ebionites in the second century. But while we cannot accept the New Testament as a trustworthy history of the early Church, nevertheless, such history may, in great part, be found there provided the reader has his eyes sharpened by the Hegelian philosophy, to see what is "between the lines."

No reader of sufficient breadth and culture to grasp Bauer's construction, can fail to see that it is a most ingenious and powerful attempt to eliminate the supernatural from Christianity, to explain its origin by connecting it with previous systems of thought, and to reduce its history to the level of a simple historical evolution. This construction has not here been outlined for controversial purposes. What I understand the truth of the matter to be, I have set forth in the preceding pages.

The reader who is not familiar with the subject, may be surprised to hear so staunch a believer as Christlieb speaking in such respectful terms of so decided a skeptic as Bauer. But Bauer is entitled to the eulogium, apart from the respect always due to ability, learning, and weight of character. All competent authorities concede that he rendered valuable service to ecclesiastical history. He had the great merit of seeing more clearly than any writer who had gone before him, that the Gospel was not an unrelated fact; that it stood in a certain definite relation to previous systems of thought; and that the orthodox Christian consciousness, so far from being an instantaneous creation, was an evolution. He gave a new importance to some passages of the New Testament, reading into them a new meaning, and throwing them into new relations. Even orthodox Church historians will never again write Church History just as they were accustomed to write it previous to his great labors. Bauer's capital mistakes are: (1.) The denial of the supernatural; (2.) An exaggeration of the influence of older systems in producing Christianity, and of human agents in determining its development; (3.) A similar exaggeration of the Jewish features of the Primitive Church, and of the conflict in the Apostolic Age.

The origin of Historical Christianity, with reference to Bauer's theories, is well discussed by Prof. G. P. Fisher, "The Supernatural Origin of Christianity," and "The Beginnings of Christianity;" by Prof. J. B. Lightfoot, "Galatians," Excursus on "St. Paul and the Three;" and by Dr. Theodore Christlieb, "Modern Doubt and Christian Belief," Eighth Lecture. I have made use of all these authorities, especially in preparing this note.

www.ingramcontent.com/pod-product-compliance
Lightning Source LLC
Chambersburg PA
CBHW020146170426
43199CB00010B/908